Behind The Walls
I Called Home

Doretha Brown-Simmons

Donna
Remember God
is aways with
you. Doretha Brown Simmons

ISBN-13: 978-1987790658

ISBN-10: 1987790650

DEDICATION

*I*n memory of my beloved husband

Mr. Willie Simmons

*"Your life will not play out like you want.
But the one who writes a better story
will be with you in every trial."*

~John Piper

CONTENTS

*"Put your hope in the LORD.
Travel steadily along his path. He will
honor you by giving you the land."*

—Psalm 37:34 NLT

ACKNOWLEDGMENTS

First, I thank God for placing the desire in my heart to write my testimony and the vision to turn it into a book that would encourage others to place their hope in God. Second, I'd like to thank all my friends and family members who were very supportive in seeing me give birth to *Behind The Walls I Called Home*. Third, many thanks go to Barbara Alpert for all her time and dedication that she devoted to my book. Without her steadfast help, this book would not have come to completion. Last but not least, I am very grateful to the ladies from the "Women's Writers Circle" small group and our wise saying, "As iron sharpens iron, so writers sharpen writers." I thank each one of you ladies (Barbara, Julie, Bridget, Denise, Jean) for your hands-on involvement in this project. Your time, prayers, support, editing, revisions, and witnessing each of you bring your manuscripts to publication encouraged me to keep writing and believing that *Behind The Walls I Called Home* would be published too.

"Grace is when God gives us good things that we don't deserve.
Mercy is when He spares us from things we deserve.
Blessings are when He is generous with both.
Truly, we can never run out of reasons to thank Him."

~Author Unknown

1

THE FIRST PLACE I CALLED HOME

As I sit here reminiscing about my past, I thank God for all that He has done in my life. Miraculously, He has brought me through, over, and around many rough terrains. There were times when I thought I wouldn't make it, but somehow He sheltered, provided, and made a way for me to get through each episode. I grew up in poverty, surrounded by drugs, alcohol, and violence. As an innocent little girl, I thought that was the ordinary way of life.

At the age of four, I witnessed my mom being beaten by my stepfather. She braced herself under the kitchen table, caged in by the chairs, trying to escape his violent hands. Her cries and frightening screams for help went unheard. I peeked around the wall just enough to see what was happening but hid enough so I wouldn't be next. This occurrence, and others like it, were never mentioned or talked about as though they had never happened. The police were never called. I soon realized that this abnormality was "normal"—at least in my life.

My saving grace was Sunday mornings. No matter what went on behind the walls I called home, on Sunday mornings Mom dressed my younger brother Curtis and me to take us to church. I am blessed to say that I learned about God at a very early age. My understanding was that if I prayed and believed in God, He would save me from all my troubles. I remember talking to God almost constantly. It was my way of escaping the chaos around me.

I still remember a great deal from the age of four, retracing the very day I sat on the floor playing with my dolls trying to stay away from angry hands. Mom approached me and mentioned that I would be starting school. The school she enrolled me in was known as Head Start, a preschool program for low-income families. I remember that first day of school so precisely—entering my classroom in the white portable building. It seemed like there were children everywhere. I must have started midway in the school year because I was introduced to all the other kids there. There were two to three teachers assigned to the class at all times. The room was brightly painted and was full of fun things to do. I felt safe and happy there.

Our day started off by first brushing our teeth. The first time I ever brushed my teeth was in that classroom. All the students lined up and took turns brushing their teeth at the sink. I had watched Mom brush her teeth at home many times, and now I was ready for it to be my turn. The sound of mom's toothbrush while she brushed always caught my attention. When my teacher placed toothpaste on my toothbrush and handed it to me, I brushed vigorously trying to make the same sound Mom did when she brushed her teeth, but I didn't hear anything. I rinsed my mouth out like I saw the other children do and then went off to tend to the rest of the school day. Our day consisted of an orderly routine of breakfast time, teaching time, story time, play time, lunch time, and nap time. All of these activities are a typical day in Head Start.

Once a week we had "circle time." The teachers sat us in a circle, and we shared with one another about our weekends. When it was my turn, I shared about the fights that I saw at home. When Mom arrived to pick me up on those days, I noticed one of my teachers would bring her outside to talk with her. When we returned home, I was hit several times by her angry hands, but never understood why. I soon realized that saying the wrong things during circle time upset her. I very quickly learned to stop sharing during circle time.

I learned that what happened *behind the walls I called home* wasn't to be mentioned to anyone. Even though I did not say anything during circle time anymore, which was okay, preschool was still a safe haven for me. I often prayed and talked to God there. I prayed about everything. He was the only one whom I trusted in to keep my secrets. I always felt better when I whispered my hurts to Him.

Besides going to school, the rest of my day was spent inside the walls I called home. It was an older wooden house with an enormous screened-in front porch. I spent most of my time there, playing with dolls and gazing outside, fascinated by the chickens roaming around our fenced-in yard. We had one rooster that must have thought he was a dog. The rare times I traveled outside alone, he would fan down one side of his long feathers, dragging them to the ground, and would chase me all over the yard like he was having a field day. Needless to say, his bad temper made me afraid to go outside alone.

My two brothers lived at home with us. Curtis was only a year old and was too young to play with me. And my older brother Bob, who was nearing seventeen, was too old to play with me. He was seldom home in the evening hours. However, the precious time Bob and I did spend together was at the beginning of each school day when he walked me to school. Bob was very patient and calm with me. He never seemed to be upset or angry. He never made me feel like I was a bother or a "handful." My school was near Tropicana, an orange juice factory in Bradenton, Florida. I loved the aroma of the oranges on my way to school. We passed by so many houses. However, many of them looked abandoned, but people lived in them.

There was one house we passed by that didn't look as run down and abandoned as other houses on the street. That particular house always had beautiful flowers all over the yard. On the front porch of that house sat an older lady who yelled at Bob and me every day.

She would either yell, "You better not step in my yard!" or "Get off my yard!" No matter how far we stayed away from her yard, she always yelled at us.

Bob never said anything back to her. He just made sure I was okay. I always felt safe around Bob, as though God had given me my personal bodyguard, a real Guardian Angel.

I wondered if he knew what life was like at home when he wasn't there in the evening. Although Mom and my stepdad lived in the same house, it seemed like they were separated. There was never much interaction between the adults and the children in that home. We never had play time or "mommy and me" time. They always seemed busy, a great deal of which I observed from a safe distance. When Mom brought me home from school, she was busy caring for Curtis and preparing meals, as though I did not exist.

My stepfather had something interesting about him. It seemed like he could fix anything that was broken except his broken heart. He would do all sorts of different things to any broken machine. Somehow he magically made them all work again. I often observed him fixing things outside as I sat on our screened-in front porch playing with my dolls and watching him—but only when he wasn't looking. I recognized any eye contact with him or Mom would upset them, so I tried my best not to look at them. For hours, he would be working on stuff in the yard, yet that crazy rooster never chased after him. I waited for that day to happen, but it never did.

On rare occasions, my stepdad and Mom brought Curtis and me to a popular shopping center located in our town. Back in the late seventies, it was called Cortez Plaza. There were a lot of stores there. We window shopped. After browsing around, we loaded into the car and drove to a place called ABC Liquor store. Then we parked under a tree where Mom and my stepdad sat and drank while Curtis and I watched from the back seat.

The only other thing we did together as a family was each summer, for a week, everyone except Bob went to South Carolina where most of Mom's side of the family lived. My grandma, aunts, uncles, and cousins lived there. Those were the times I saw Mom at her happiest—in Grandma's little wooden house that had two small bedrooms, a living room, and a tiny kitchen that had a small kerosene stove. Grandma's house didn't have an inside bathroom. She had what was called an outhouse, which consisted of just a toilet and a roll of toilet paper. It reminded me of a "porta-potty" but not as fancy. It was made out of wood and was located in the backyard a short distance from the house.

Grandma's house sat about a mile from the highway, on a narrow dirt road leading to the house. The whole area was surrounded by cornfields. Whenever my mom, aunts, and uncles gathered they were always excited. Everyone talked at the same time, but somehow they communicated with one another. Grandma was the very calm one of the bunch. I never heard her raise her voice. There was an overabundance of peace about her—flowing from her. I was told my grandfather was much older than she was. He had passed away when Mom was about ten years old. The only thing I knew about him was that whenever he went to the bathroom, his urine was red with blood. I never knew my grandfather's diagnosis.

As time passed, my kindergarten and first-grade years were not that much different from my preschool year. Life at home was the same. The two places I always felt safe were at school and church. During those years, I was old enough to sing in the children's choir at church. I loved it. I thanked God that Mom faithfully took me to church. I believe she needed church time to escape everything else, just like me. I don't think anyone at church was aware of the battles we faced behind the walls we called home. If Mom wanted me to stay quiet around others, she probably stayed quiet around her church family too.

Doretha Brown-Simmons

"You are my hiding place; you will protect me from trouble and surround me with songs of deliverance."

—Psalm 32:7 NIV

2

MY SCHOOL HOME

My second-grade year was out of the ordinary. We never really had visitors in our home, but that particular year my cousin George often came to visit us from Miami. He was in his mid-twenties, and tall. He always wore a suit. The other thing that changed for me that year was that I was bused to a new elementary school that was miles away from my home. That was my first year riding a school bus. I soon realized on the bus ride to school that some kids could be cruel. One particular girl, who was older than I, stood out the most. She scorned me, poked me and pulled my barrettes out of my hair.

I told her several times, "Please, stop!" or "Please leave me alone." But that only made matters worse.

I learned it was best not to say anything. I just kept silent and told no one. Some of the kids on the bus were entertained by her actions. She succeeded in making me afraid of her.

One day while exiting the bus she pushed me off, causing me to land on the concrete ground. I laid there in so much pain because one of my legs was injured severely. When Mom and my stepdad arrived at the bus stop, they had to carry me to the car. They immediately drove me to the hospital. That was my first trip to the emergency room. There I was fitted with a soft cast-like covering and was handed crutches to help me walk. Learning how to walk with them was an adventure. It took a lot of practice, patience, and perseverance, but after tumbling over several times and getting back up each time, I finally got the hang of them. I wondered if the girl who bullied me, felt like she accomplished a goal because she constantly bragged about what she did. She was truly a prime example of a bully. I often wondered if she was abused by someone in her life, and bullying me was her way of trying to build up her self-confidence.

The same year, on a typical bus ride to school, things suddenly changed. The bus driver did not stop to pick up Alex. That was odd because he always got on the bus. He never missed school. When we arrived at school, we were informed that Alex wouldn't be in our class anymore. Apparently, while he was playing near his house, trying to catch a frog, he fell into the pond and drowned. We were told that he died. That was a painful day for me. I often told God how much I missed Alex. Alex was my friend.

Shortly after school let out for the summer, Mom approached me with a letter in her hand. Looking down at me she calmly said, "You did not pass to the third grade."

I burst into tears when I heard this shocking news. I loved school and thought I did great in all my classes, but the letter in her hand said otherwise. My best was just not good enough. The thought of not going onto third grade made me feel like I had a dunce hat on my head. I thought I had done something wrong—again.

During that same time, Cousin George returned for another visit. His stop-overs always had a way of brightening up the atmosphere in our home. It became a custom to see Cousin George wearing a suit. The only time I ever witnessed men wearing suits was on Sunday mornings at church. However, Cousin George was an exception: he wore suits every day, all day. He always seemed to be on a mission of some sort. He was always up to doing something good for us. This time, he was there to help Mom and Bob move our belongings out of the house that we had called home.

3

A NEW PLACE CALLED HOME

At first, I did not understand what was happening. Everything took place so quickly; as though it was "in the twinkling of an eye." Because we were in a hurry to get out quickly, we did not bring much with us. In the midst of this sudden move, I grabbed my dolls. I carried them because I didn't want any of them to be left behind. With George's help, Mom, Bob, Curtis and I settled into a two bedroom duplex apartment. My stepdad did not move with us; Mom left him behind. I believe God sent Cousin George to help get us out of a dangerous situation. Once his mission was completed, Cousin George returned to his normal life in Miami, and we started a new life in the duplex I soon called home.

Due to the move, I started the school year at a different school. I counted it a blessing because the students were unaware that I was repeating second grade. However, I was obviously taller than the kids in my class, and they reminded me of it quite often. I was ashamed to talk about being held back, and I hoped my classmates wouldn't find out.

I continuously prayed, "God, please help me with my schoolwork. I don't want to be held back in second grade again." I say "continuously" instead of "continually," because continually indicates the stop and then start of the same event. It's an important distinction. I prayed this prayer everyday throughout second grade. I was determined not to be held back, again!

To make ends meet, both Mom and Bob worked. Also during that time, Curtis started kindergarten. I loved being his big sister. We enjoyed walking to and from school together. The school was nearly two miles from our home. Whenever we walked to or from school, I tightly held his little hand. I made sure that we stayed away from passing cars. I felt it was my mission to keep him safe, like my big brother Bob had kept me safe when he walked me to school when I was younger.

After school, we walked to a nearby neighbor's house. He looked after us until Mom finished work. I had no idea what type of relationship they had. I don't even remember him coming to our home. Mom drove to his house after work to pick my brother and me up. Before going home, they sat and socialized, drinking beer and other alcohol. He drank with Mom often. During those times, Curtis and I were allowed to go outside to play with the other kids. He was much older than Mom, with grandchildren the age of Curtis and me.

As time went on, he became interested in me. It wasn't in a good, healthy way. When no one was around, he demanded that Curtis go outside to play, while he ordered me to stay inside. He commanded me to drink from his beer can.

"It's good for you," he told me.

I remember gulping some of it down. I wanted to spit it out because it tasted like bitter ginger ale. However, I refrained from doing it out of fear that he would get angry with me. Then he demanded I sit on the couch and lie down next to him. He soon began touching me in uncomfortable places and ordered me to do things to him that I did not feel comfortable doing. His threatening-looking face frightened me. I was eight years old, and I was very scared.

With a firm voice, he told me, "This is our secret. Don't tell anyone." When responding back to adults, I was trained to say "yes, sir" and "yes, ma'am."

So I answered with, "Yes sir," and did as I was told. Being raised at a young age to be silent, I didn't tell anyone. I remained mute about what he was doing to me.

Since the move, we didn't go to church anymore. But I had God in my heart and talked to Him often. Because I felt trapped and alone in this sad situation, I spoke to God about the pain I was experiencing when that dirty old man invaded my body. Sadly, this went on for over a year. Talking to God about it was my only relief. God was my safe haven.

My saving grace arrived when Mom decided to move to South Carolina in 1982. I was midway through third grade. She took Curtis and me with her, but my older brother Bob stayed in Florida. I was sad to leave Bob, but being taken away from the cruel man who was sexually abusing me was a blessing. He wouldn't be able to hurt me anymore. This was proof that God wasn't only *listening* to my prayers, but was *answering* them too. He had provided a way to snatch me out of the hands of that perverted man, and I praised Him for my deliverance. Even though I was pulled out of the situation, I still carried the degrading memories for a very long time.

"In my distress I prayed to the LORD, and the LORD answered me and set me free."

—Psalm 118:5 NLT

4

ANOTHER PLACE CALLED HOME

*W*e moved in with my grandma, Aunt Rose (Mom's youngest sister), and two uncles. It was unbelievable how all seven of us managed to cram into Grandma's tiny little house, the same house with the outhouse in the back yard that we had visited in the past. This way of life was foreign to me. There was no indoor plumbing. The water that was used came from an outside well. It was hand pumped out of a cast iron, antique water pump that was secured in the ground. The iron pipe, where the water came out of, stood about four feet tall and was located near Grandma's garden. Uncle Eddie was responsible for pumping the water for the family. He would pump tubs of water at a time.

The majority of what we ate came out of Grandma's garden. Laundry was done on the front porch in a large round tin tub. They used a huge bar of laundry soap. The soap was about three or four times the size of a bar of bath soap. Grandma, Mom and Aunt Rose used separate tin tubs. They rubbed the soap on every piece of clothes and then scrubbed the clothes on a washboard. The clothes were then hung on the clothesline to dry. The same large tin tubs were used for baths.

The garbage man did not come and pick up our trash, as they did when I lived in Florida. The trash was burned in an area in the backyard. Trash-burning time was fascinating.

Six-year-old Curtis always clung to Mom's side even when she did her chores—except for during trash-burning time. That was the only time besides going to school that he did not cling to Mom. He would stand alone at a safe distance, mesmerized by the flames. It was interesting watching him look at the trash burn. I wonder what was on his mind as he stood there staring so steadfastly.

One day while we were settled in on Grandma's front porch, an unfamiliar blue car drove up. Mom, Grandma, Aunt Rose, and Uncle Eddie stood on the porch. They all gazed speechlessly, standing stock still, as the car approached the house. The car seemed to drive slowly, probably due to all the lumps and bumps in that long dirt road. The car finally arrived in the yard.

A woman and a man got out of the car along with a tall young man that looked very much like my older brother Bob, who still lived in Florida. He had big bright eyes, a very light skin tone, dark wavy hair, and a dimple in his chin just like Bob's.

I was so confused looking at him and envisioning my older brother. I was wondering why everyone seemed so shocked when the group approached the house. I was even more confused when the young man addressed my mom as "Mom."

The woman that exited the car with them, he also called "Mom." The man that got out of the car with them, he called "Pops." When the young man spoke, he had more of a southern "proper" type of accent compared to my older brother Bob in Florida. Other than that he was like a clone of my older brother.

I soon realized that he was my brother too, at least, when he was nine. Mom explained, "This is your brother Terry, your Aunt Lenora, and your Uncle Henry. They've raised Terry since he was a baby."

Aunt Lenora was Mom's older sister, and Uncle Henry was Aunt Lenora's husband. Aunt Lenora and Mom had the same father but different mothers. I was told that my grandfather was married and had several children from his first marriage. His first wife had died, and he eventually married my grandma. So much was unveiled that day.

God had blessed me with a brother that reminded me so much of my older brother in Florida. No words could express how joyful and stunned I was, finding out that I had not one, but *two* older brothers. Mom told me years later that she was very young when she gave birth to my older brother and a couple of years later gave birth to Terry. She said that she was encouraged to give Terry to Lenora and her husband. They didn't have any children, and they wanted him.

Mom also said, "They took him and did a good job raising him." She also told me that she had explained to Terry why she had to give him to Lenora and Henry. She said he understood. Mom didn't have another child until eleven years later, and that child was me.

Life went on at Grandma's house. I recall adventuring around in the yard a lot. I pulled vegetables out of Grandma's garden and ate them raw. My favorite vegetable was the turnip root. I would pull it out of the ground and wipe it off on my clothes. The turnip was a lovely purple color on the top part, and the rest of it was a whitish color. It was sort of round, and I loved the crunch. It was not sweet, but it was a little tart and *good*.

On a hot sunny day when the trash was burning, Curtis stood at a safe distance from the burn pile, as usual, mesmerized by the flames. On that particular day, I became more adventurous. I noticed a foil pie pan near the burning trash. I got it and decided to cook corn in it. I went to the corn field and pulled off the biggest ear I could find. The husks of all the corn were tan. I recalled that the only time the grown-ups cooked the corn was when the outer covering was green. The ear I had just picked was different—it was tan. It also had sticky, thready strands on the cob that I had to pull off to get the kernels off the cob. The kernels were hard as a rock. I plucked them off one by one and put them in my foil pan. By the time I was ready to cook my corn the fire on the trash pile had gone out. Fortunately, there was a little black log on the edge of the burned pile of ashes that was still red hot. It was the perfect place to cook my corn. I set my pan on that hot log. I watched and watched and watched. My corn didn't look like it was cooking. Suddenly, to my amazement, the corn started bouncing in the pan and started splitting open. My hard little dried up kernels turned into popcorn! I jumped around with such excitement, as much as the popped corn popped all over the place. There were more kernels on the ground than in my pan. I somehow got my pan off the hot log. I shared what I had with my brother. I was so proud of myself. I had made popcorn!

I spent most of my time entertaining myself. The only time Curtis and I were around other children was in school or when my Aunt Lois (Mom's other younger sister) and my cousins, Nicole and Tammy came to visit. Nicole was one year younger than I, and Tammy was about five years older. Nicole and I had so much in common. I remember we would laugh and play hopscotch and pretend that we were cheerleaders. We talked, and we giggled a lot. When they came to visit, I always enjoyed being around them. I admired how they were always so nicely dressed from head to toe. Their hair was always done so picture-perfect, with barrettes and shoes matching their outfits. I realize that I did not have as much as they had. At school also, it was plainly evident that I did not have much.

I do believe Mom did the best she could during that time in our life. She was unemployed. For Christmas that year, we each received one gift. Curtis received a toy police car with flashing red lights on the top. It spun around in circles and made siren noises. I received a pack of jacks with a little bouncy ball that came with them. The price on the pack was one dollar and ninety-nine cents.

I enjoyed watching that fascinating little toy police car that kept my brother so well entertained as I sat near him playing with my jacks and ball. I would bounce the ball and pick up jacks over and over again. I thank God for that Christmas. We did not get a lot, but we both were blessed with that one gift, and we cherished it.

The town we lived in with Grandma was a small town called Pinewood, South Carolina. I understand how Pinewood received its name. It was surrounded by tall pine trees all over the place. Pinewood had a couple of small general stores that sold food, and a small supply store. The supply store sold things like parts for the antique water pump, kerosene lamps, cast iron pans, tin tubs, and used furniture. We rarely went shopping. We probably went once a month, and it was fun. Everyone in town seemed to know one other. It was a meeting place for the adults to socialize.

When we did go to the store, our first stop was the general store next to the supply store. That was my favorite place because we got ice cream. My number one choice was the double scoop cone of butter pecan ice cream, which was also Mom's favorite. We sat together on the bench outside the general store and ate our ice cream.

Mom, Grandma, Aunt Rose, and Uncle Eddie spent most of their time talking with other grown-ups. I overheard them talking about *The Possum Trot Festival* in May. I heard it talked about several times. I didn't clearly understand what it was, but I was curious about what it was all about. I knew what "playing possum" meant. It meant a person or animal pretended to be dead. But that was all I knew about possums. I had no idea how a possum looked or what a Possum Trot Festival was. I knew when I was sitting on that bench eating ice cream and listening, I wanted to go because everyone else seemed so happy about going. It was the talk of the town.

After we had finished our ice cream and everyone ended their conversations we went into the supply store. I enjoyed walking around and looking at all the different gadgets for sale there. It was not a coincidence that one particular man was always buying something when we were there. He was known as "the new man in town." He was quiet, and it seemed like he was a stranger to everyone. He would smile at Mom, and she would return his smile.

Several months later, we were on our routine trip, buying ice cream, sitting on the bench, and shopping at the supply store, the "new man in town" walked in while we were shopping. He not only smiled at Mom, but he also approached her. They talked for the first time outside the store. He eventually started visiting Mom at Grandma's house.

I always felt nervous around him. I was praying that Mom would not leave me alone with him. I was scared that he would invade my body and touch me in uncomfortable places, the way her other friend in Florida did. Time went on. Mom continued talking to the man, and we went to visit him at his home often. I thanked God that Mom didn't leave me alone with him. Curtis and I liked going to his house because he lived near the store. He would give my brother and I each a handful of coins. We were so excited, and wasting no time, we dashed out of the house and headed for the store.

There was a train track across the street from his house. My brother and I raced on the train track all the way to the store. We bought candy, eating most of it before arriving back to his house. One day when Curtis and I got our handfuls of coins, we decided to put our money together to buy a watermelon. There were watermelons lined up in one corner of the store. They costed two dollars each. My brother and I put all of our coins on the counter and Mr. Johnny told us that we could pick any one we wanted.

I was thrilled that we had a choice. I chose the biggest watermelon I had ever seen. I could barely pick it up. I staggered back to the house carrying that gigantic watermelon. I sat it down several times on our trip back down the railroad track. I needed to *rest*. My brother tagged along looking helpless because he was not able to carry it. We finally arrived at the house. Mom cut the watermelon open for us. When she opened the watermelon, it was overripe and didn't taste like a watermelon. I learned a lesson that day: bigger is not always better.

May finally arrived, and with it the Possum Trot Festival. I was nine years old and in fourth grade. My Teacher, Mrs. Griffin, explained to me what the festival was. She said that Pinewood was known as "The Home of The Possum Trot Festival." Each year in May, the small town hosted the traditional festival. People came from near and far to enjoy the festivities. Mrs. Griffin was right. There were people everywhere. On the day of the event, it was jaw-dropping to see how many people could be crammed into our small town. There was so much food and so many rides to enjoy. The most favorite food, of course, was the possum. Everyone looked like they were having the time of their lives.

But Mom didn't look like she was having the time of her life. She looked weak and tired. She constantly said, "I need to sit down." I distinctly remember her telling my Aunt Rose, "Rose, I am so sick. I'm ready to go home."

It was my first time at the festival. I had always heard others talk about it and being there was better than I imagined. I was there for a short period, and I had so much fun. But I didn't understand how sick Mom was. I was all caught up in the excitement as was everyone else. On our way back to Grandma's house I was praying that Mom would feel better soon. Mom had probably been sick for a while and just couldn't hide it any longer. When we arrived home, Mom went to bed.

Mom must have gone to the doctor because one evening she sat us down on the front porch. She told us that she would be going into the hospital in a few days to have surgery. She didn't go into details about what type of surgery. She just basically said that after her surgery, she would feel better again. She told us we would be staying with Aunt Lenora, Terry, and Uncle Henry until she felt better. I was glad God had heard my prayer to help Mom feel better, and I was happy to be going to stay with Aunt Lenora, Terry and Uncle Henry again.

Doretha Brown-Simmons

*"Every miracle begins with a problem,
and every problem presents an opportunity for
Christ to help us in our difficulty."*

~Dr. David Jerimiah

5

A DIFFERENT PLACE CALLED HOME

The next day Terry came to Grandma's house to pick us up. He loaded our belongings into the car. Curtis was six years old at that time and seemed unsure about what was happening. But he came along as he was told.

We finally arrived at their red brick house. It was much bigger than Grandma's house. When we entered the front door, we were greeted by Aunt Lenora and Uncle Henry in their living room. Their kitchen was located near the living room, and it had a stove with an oven, a kitchen table with chairs, and lots of kitchen cabinets. Down the hall, they had a full bathroom with a sink, toilet, bathtub, and shower. Near the bathroom were three bedrooms.

Their house reminded me of the duplex apartment where we had lived in Florida, but it was much bigger and nicer. They had a large garden in the back yard twice the size of Grandma's garden. There were lots of tomatoes, cabbage, collard greens, string beans, and okra. But, sadly, they didn't have turnips. On the opposite side of their backyard was a hog pen with big hogs that made grunting sounds and waddled in the mud. They had a lot of space in the hog pen, but the hogs always seemed to huddle together. Uncle Henry was usually busy working in the garden and caring for the pigs. When I asked him questions about the hogs, he enthusiastically explained or answered my questions. Curtis and I received so much attention, and everyone seemed so happy that we were there. That was the first time I had positive, genuine interaction with adults outside of school.

My brother Terry was about twenty years old. He helped take care of us. I remember him combing and styling my hair, washing our clothes, and introducing us to his friends. I was blessed with the opportunity to finally get to know my other big brother. He worked as a radio broadcaster. Aunt Lenora had his radio station on in the living room. I would sit and stare at the radio for hours, fascinated by the sound of my brother's voice.

Aunt Lenora would call me into the kitchen when she prepared dinner. I watched and helped. I felt so special. I had never been allowed in the kitchen while the adults were cooking before. But Aunt Lenora didn't start until I was in the kitchen with her. She would explain everything to me as I watched and listened. She would tell me about the ingredients she used in the food and why she used it. Sugar is used in deserts to make it taste sweet. Flour is used for baking and making the batter. Sprinkling salt and pepper on vegetables and meats improve the flavors. Her macaroni and cheese were my favorite. She boiled the macaroni, and then drained the water off into the sink. Next, she put the macaroni in a casserole dish, added chunks of diced cheese, milk, butter, salt, and pepper. I helped mix and stir the ingredients together as she instructed; then she placed it in the preheated oven. The oven had a window. I stared through the window, waiting for it to finish cooking. The food seemed to cook faster when I didn't stare at it, but I could not resist. I helped prepare it, so I was proud of myself as I watched it bake. When the macaroni and cheese turned slightly brown on the top, it was done. The thought of it makes my mouth water even now. If gold were food, it would probably taste like Aunt Lenora's macaroni and cheese.

I felt like an important person when I was in Aunt Lenora's presence. She seemed to love her role as my aunt. Aunt Lenora was the first woman in my life that told me I did an excellent job. Simple words like that meant so much. I felt so special at her house. I was able to look at Aunt Lenora eye to eye, without any fear.

Mom didn't give me compliments and looking at her eye to eye made her angry. Aunt Lenora never yelled or hit me with violent, angry hands. Their home was pleasant and so peaceful. I never saw or heard Aunt Lenora or Uncle Henry argue or fight. God showed me peace, love, and kindness through them. Terry enjoyed this house that he called home. Aunt Lenora was proud to be his mom.

I remember sitting and watching her ironing his clothes with a beam of joy on her face. Every piece of his clothing was ironed to perfection. Pictures of Terry were all around the living room. Uncle Henry was proud to be his Pops. They often talked and laughed together. I admired the many times we gathered in the living room watching television or looking at picture books. I experienced a new way of life when I was with them.

Uncle Henry devoted a lot of time to caring for the hogs and the garden. He sold the hogs and vegetables. I understood why their garden was bigger than Grandma's garden. They needed enough to eat and enough left over to sell. Aunt Lenora canned— which we called "jarred"—tomatoes from the garden. When it was time to jar the tomatoes, Uncle Henry brought a couple of buckets of plump red tomatoes into the kitchen. Aunt Lenora prepared to jar them. She washed the tomatoes then placed them in boiling water. She explained that when she boiled them for a few minutes, it made them easier to peel. That was incredible to see how the skin slipped right off. She used a particular type of jar that was made just for jarring foods. She stuffed the peeled tomatoes in the jar and placed the top on it.

I asked, "Why do you jar the tomatoes?"

She answered, "I jar them for the winter." She called it "winter food."

My younger brother Curtis went home, back to Grandma's house a month later. I told God that I was not ready to go back to Grandma's house. Mom was home and feeling better, but I wanted to stay longer, and that was okay with Aunt Lenora, Mom, and everyone else. So we took my brother back home, riding in the back of Uncle Henry's red pickup truck. Curtis and I enjoyed the ride in the back of the truck. I loved sitting in the back and feeling the breeze on my face.

I was glad to see Mom was feeling better, but I was most

excited that she allowed me to stay with my aunt and uncle a little longer. I thanked God for answering my prayer. I enjoyed going places with Aunt Lenora when she ran errands. My three favorite places were her friend's house, the grocery store, and the gas station. She did everything in one trip. I was told the day before when she planned to go anywhere. Aunt Lenora was very organized and structured. She moved around a little slow sometimes, because she had issues with her knees, but that didn't stop her. I thank God for giving her the strength to do all the things she did with me.

First we would visit her friend. She was an older lady with beautiful snow white hair. She lived in a big white wooden house with a large yard. The yard had lots of pecan trees, but there were no pecans on them. Aunt Lenora told me that the pecans were harvested in the winter. Surrounding the large yard were vast soybean fields that reached as far as my eyes could see.

The house and yard were always filled with her grandchildren. There were little ones in diapers, children old enough to play with me, and teenagers. Our favorite game was hide-and-seek. We started the game by rounding up everyone that wanted to play. We all gathered together at the counting post, which was one of the large pecan trees in the front yard. I waited with a little dance in my step, as I anticipated who would count first. The oldest child counted to choose who was it, "one potato, two potato, three potato, out," until one person was left. That person would be "it."

I liked to count, and to hide—I loved everything about the game. When I was "it" I was proud. I faced the tree, crossed my arms and held them up to cover my eyes as I leaned on the tree. I counted as loud as I could "one-two-three-four-five-six-seven-eight-nine-ten, ready or not here I come!"

I marched away from my counting post like I was on a mission. I was ready to tag everyone. When I stepped away from the tree, many of them ran out of nowhere and touched home base, which meant they were safe. There was always one or two that were hard to find. When I finally found or caught someone to tag, the game was finished. We played the game over and over until Aunt Lenora told me it was time to leave.

Next we would go to the grocery store. The store we shopped at was a called Piggly Wiggly. The logo of the shop was a jolly, happy-faced pig. Pigs and hogs seemed popular in that area.

The store was much bigger than the general store in Pinewood. The town they lived in was Manning, South Carolina, much larger than Pinewood. The stores had grocery carts, many varieties of foods, and lots of people working there. They didn't sell my favorite double scoop butter pecan ice cream cone. They sold ice cream and ice cream cones, but they were sold separately. They did have my favorite cereal "Captain Crunch." Yummy.

That store had everything that Aunt Lenora had on her list. I helped her shop. The two most important things I remembered were not to place anything on the bread because the bread would lose its shape. Smashed bread made very awkward sandwiches and toast. The eggs could crack if not handled carefully. I was very careful with the bread and with the cartoon of eggs. The canning jars were secured in a box. Aunt Lenora handled the box. I helped with rest of the groceries that were easier to handle. When we finished shopping, we loaded up the car and journeyed on to our next place. Our final stop was the gas station. We passed several gas stations, but Aunt Lenora always went to the one closer to her home. The gas station was called Texaco.

I liked going there because she gave me the money to pay for the gas while she waited at the gas pump. I stood in line like everyone else and kept my eye on Aunt Lenora at the same time. One day when we stopped for gas. Aunt Lenora gave me a twenty-dollar bill to pay for ten dollars of regular gas.

I handed the money to the cashier and said, "Ten dollars' worth of regular gas please, for the blue car."

He took the twenty-dollar bill and gave me a twenty-dollar bill as my change. I walked to the door with the money in my hand and paused. I thought to myself, *What would God want me to do?* I turned around went back to the cashier and said, "You gave me too much money back. I need only ten dollars."

He took the twenty dollar bill back and gave me a ten dollar bill back. I told Aunt Lenora what happened. She smiled and placed the change in her purse. I knew I had done the right thing, and I was proud of myself.

One day Uncle Henry and Terry were preparing to go for a ride. Terry asked if I wanted to ride along. I said, "Yes!", before he finished the question. I never passed up an opportunity to ride in the back of Uncle Henry's pickup truck. I sat in the back of the truck alone. The ride was nice, and the view was picture perfect. Suddenly, out of nowhere, I began thinking about Curtis and Mom. I think I was getting home sick, but I didn't say anything.

Uncle Henry stopped his truck in the middle of the road. Terry stepped out of the truck to remove a turtle from the road. He picked it up. The turtle was the size of his hand.

"Can I have that turtle?" I asked excitedly. "Please, can I have it?"

Terry brought it to the back of the truck so that I could get a closer look. It had a hard grayish, black shell with a tinge of yellow on the bottom part of it. The turtle's face was coarse looking. Terry probably figured if I looked at it close-up, I would change my mind. He asked, "You want this?"

"Yes!" I answered, my eyes wide.

When we arrived home, I flew into the house. I found Aunt Lenora in her room folding clothes.

I yelled excitedly, "Aunt Lenora! Aunt Lenora! I have a turtle! Come outside to see it!"

Uncle Henry and Terry were in the back yard, making a place for it. Aunt Lenora asked where we had gotten it. I told her that it was in the middle of the road, and we saved it from getting run over. Uncle Henry said it needed to be placed near the house so it could have shade, and an area for water so it can drink and have fun.

I asked Uncle Henry and Terry "What do turtles eat?"

They said, "Raw okra, cabbage, collard greens, apples, crickets, bugs, and earthworms."

So every day Uncle Henry diced up food and mixed it together so I could feed my turtle. And he undoubtedly liked to eat. I was told not to put my fingers near his mouth. So I was very careful when I fed him. I didn't want him to mistake my fingers for food. I named him T-Turtle, a simple name that everyone could remember. The food he ate seemed to give him a lot of energy. He was fast compared to the turtles I had seen on television. T-Turtle liked to cool off and play in his water area.

My daily routine changed after T-Turtle became my pet. He was my first pet, and I made sure to give him great care. I checked on him throughout the day, until sunset.

After bedtime prayer, I laid in bed wondering what T-Turtle was doing. I thought about him so much. I had dreams about him. When morning finally arrived, I was happy to see everyone and But I couldn't wait to go outside to feed him. I rushed to wash my face, brush my teeth and dashed into the kitchen to fix my cereal and milk. I ate quickly, so I could go outside to feed him and refill his water area. I didn't want him to be lonely. I was attached to him. I thank God for blessing me with T-Turtle.

One evening while we were all having dinner, everyone seemed unusually calm and quiet. Aunt Lenora and Terry told me that school was about to start. I knew what that meant. It was time for me to go back home to Grandma's house. They told me that I would be leaving in a week. I was sad at the thought of leaving. I wished I could be in both places at the same time. I missed Curtis and Mom, but I loved staying at Aunt Lenora's house. I was concerned about T-Turtle because I knew I could not bring him home with me.

I asked, tears filling my eyes, "What about my turtle?"

Uncle Henry said, "I have a friend that would like to take T-Turtle and give him a good home."

The thought of giving T-Turtle away made me feel like I was giving away a piece of my heart. I remember the day I told him goodbye. That was hard. I had to prepare to go back to my "normal" life at Grandma's house. I realized that I would miss all the things we did together at Aunt Lenora's and Uncle Henry's.

The adults at Grandma's house didn't interact with the kids. They supplied our basic needs, but the majority of the time I entertained myself. The day arrived for me to return to Grandma's house. Terry was at work. He told me many times that he would miss me. He reassured me that we would see each other again.

He looked into my eyes and said, "I wish you could live here with me."

I said, "I wish I could too." I thought to myself; *it would be nice if Curtis and Mom could live there with me.* I knew that was impossible.

Uncle Henry was not home either.

Aunt Lenora and I loaded my belongings in the trunk of her car. She was making sniffling sounds. Aunt Lenora was crying. I told her not to cry, and tears welled up in my eyes. She said that I was a good girl and that she'd miss me.

I said, "I'll miss you too." The trip to Grandma's house was quiet.

I was feeling sad, scared, and anxious all at the same time. I didn't know what to expect when I arrived home. When I saw the sign, that said, "Pinewood Speed Limit." I knew we were very close to Grandma's house. When I arrived, everyone was standing on the front porch. When we got out of the car, Curtis ran to my side. Mom and everyone else greeted me. I had mixed emotions. I was quiet and smiled at everyone. Aunt Lenora visited for a short time.

When she drove away, I watched her blue car until it was out of sight. I told my brother I had a pet turtle and that I had named him T-Turtle. I told him everything about T-Turtle. I described how he looked, his size, and what he liked to do. He was fascinated by the stories I told him. I wanted to show him an earthworm. We dug all around the yard until we found some. He was even more fascinated to see and hold the worm than he was with the stories of T-Turtle. We were so excited we ran up to Mom.

She reacted as if we showed her a meat-eating dinosaur. She demanded loudly, "*Do not* bring that thing near me!"

She demanded further that we put them back where we had gotten them from. I realized then that Mom was not a fan of earthworms, so my brother and I put them back on the ground where we had found them.

The new man in town, Harold, was still friends with Mom. They were together often. We stayed with him more than we stayed with Grandma. One day when Harold was at work. Mom told my brother and me that we were moving back to Florida. She said, "Harold will be moving with us."

I had been looking forward to going back to school in Pinewood and seeing all my friends again. But I was seriously unhappy about moving back to Florida. I couldn't say that to my mom. I was in denial.

One day I noticed Mom was busy packing our clothes in a cardboard box. She taped the boxes with silver duct tape. I realized then that it was real. We were really, truly moving. A week later we were on a Greyhound bus, back to Florida. When we stepped onto the crowded bus, there were a few empty seats available. I was not able to sit with Curtis, Mom, or Harold. Mom told me where to sit. I sat next to a stranger. I don't remember anything about that stranger who sat next to me, but I do remember sitting in my seat stretching my neck up high, trying to gaze out the window. I took one long, hard look back. I did not want to leave.

"The Lord is my rock and my fortress and my deliverer; My God, my strength, in whom I will trust; My shield and the horn of my salvation, my stronghold."

—Psalm 18:2 NKJV

6

MY JOURNEY TO A DIFFERENT PLACE

*T*he bus soon drove away from the home where I wanted to stay. I was busy wiping the seemingly unstoppable tears that streamed down my face. I sat and prayed a silent prayer to God, "God, please help my heart not to feel so sad. Make my tears go away."

I didn't want my mom to see the hurt on my face. I felt a sense of peace shower me from the crown of my head to the soles of my feet. God instantly wiped my tears away as I sat envisioning His presence. Instead of grief at the leaving, I was instead filled with joy at seeing Bob. I thank God for my older brother. I thank God for answered prayer. I was able to sit back and relax. I looked straight ahead with the anticipation of seeing Bob again.

The ride was very long, but I suddenly didn't mind because the seats on the bus were big and comfortable. My space became a little discovery zone. I noticed a footrest in front of me. I flipped it down with the tip of my foot and rested my feet on it. I placed my arm on the armrest and then noticed a button on the tip of the armrest. Wow! I pushed it, and my seat went back like a recliner. I got very comfortable as I laid there, and soon felt my eyelids getting very heavy. I kept them open as long as I could and eventually drifted off to sleep.

I woke up to Mom nudging my shoulder. She said, "Get up, Resa, and put your shoes on. It's time to get off the bus."

I stretched my arms up high and let out a gigantic yawn. I put my shoes on and tagged along behind them. The bus driver held my arm as I stepped off the bus. I was glad he did because I was so groggy.

I noticed that we were at a huge bus station compared to the one in South Carolina.

I asked Mom, "Where is Bob?"

She said, "We aren't there yet. We're in Savanna, Georgia." She said, "We have a layover for three hours until our next bus arrives."

There were Greyhound buses lined up everywhere, and not one of them was there to take us to Bradenton, Florida.

Curtis was so excited to see so many buses. He was jumping up and down, patting Mom's arm saying, "Mommy, look! Look at the buses! Look another one is coming! See Momma, see!"

His speech was usually unclear, but I understood every word he said. We entered the bus station; Mom held his hand as he looked back at the buses. The bus station was full of people, and there was luggage everywhere. It was quite a sight. We all sat together. After sitting for a couple of hours, most of that time I could not help but gaze at one side of the bus station. There were rows of unique little seats with tiny televisions close to them.

Harold asked us, "Would you like to watch the TV?"

"Yes, sir!" I said excitedly. He gave Curtis and me a handful of quarters. We stuffed them in our pockets and said our thanks. So Curtis and I sat together and watched the tiny televisions. The cost was twenty-five cents to watch for ten minutes. We had enough quarters to watch it for a while.

I couldn't help but notice a man lying on the floor in the corner of the bus station. There was something different about him. His clothes were dirty and worn. His brown hair and beard were long and kinky. His toes peeked out of his worn shoes.

Mom was sitting next to me. I overheard Mom say to Harold, "The man in the corner seems to be homeless."

I suddenly didn't want to watch TV anymore. I was concerned about the homeless man. I reached deep into my pocket. I had two quarters left. I held them tight in my hand; I counted to ten several times to build up my nerve to ask Mom if I could give the money to him.

Courage ready, I finally walked up to her and asked, "May I please give this to the man over there?" I held out the two quarters I still held in my hand and used my other hand to point my finger barely towards the direction of the man lying in the corner.

Mom responded exactly as I expected. She said, "No! Don't even go over there. Sit down!" I returned to my seat.

Moments later Harold walked up to me and said in a very calm tone, "Give me your quarters, I will give them to him for you." I handed the coins to Harold and watched him as he walked up to the man and gave him the coins. He said something to Harold.

Harold walked back up to me and said, "Thank you."

I smiled. I thanked God for what Harold had done for me.

The man sat up, and then he stood up. He walked up to the vending machine and bought a snack. He returned to his corner, eating his snack. He finished it very fast. It was obvious that he was hungry. I was so happy that I had helped that homeless man in the corner.

I heard over the intercom, "All passengers going to Tampa, St. Petersburg, Bradenton, and Sarasota, Florida—please line up and have your tickets in your hands." That announcement was music to my ears. We gathered our belongings and quickly rushed to the line. Mom held our tickets in her hand. I prayed that two empty seats were available so Curtis and I could sit side-by-side. When we got onto the bus, Mom chose our seats. She told Curtis and me to sit together. She and Harold sat together in the seats behind us. I sat near the window and watched the rest of the people board the bus. When all the passengers were seated, the bus driver made an announcement.

He introduced himself and said, "Good evening everyone. I want to remind you that you cannot bring any weapons on this bus, no smoking, or drinking alcoholic beverages." He confirmed the destination of his route, then sat and buckled up in for the drive.

The window seat was a great spot. I enjoyed staring down at

the people in their cars. Many of the people especially children in the back seats, stared at the bus as it passed them. I smiled and waved at people in several different cars. No one waved back. I soon figured out that they didn't see me waving because the tinted windows on the bus were too dark.

I focused my attention on the air conditioner vent. It was lined along the bottom trim of the window. I held my face close to the vent and deeply inhaled the cold air as it blew on my face. When I think of it now, I vividly remember the cool breeze on my face and the smell of the air. When my face felt too ice-cold, I turned my attention to my brother.

He was preoccupied, playing with his toy car. I asked him to park his toy car in between us because I wanted to show him how unique his seat was. His legs were too short to reach his foot rest, but he thought the button on the armrest was fun. He pressed it way more than I expected. He was going up and down like a rocking chair moving in slow motion.

Mom tapped him on the arm then peeped at him from the seat behind us and said, "Curtis, stop playing with that. It is not a toy."

He halted abruptly in a laid-back position. He smiled at me, and I slightly smiled back. My goal was not to make Mom mad at him. He laid back, held his toy car and soon drifted off to sleep. I began to sightsee out my window. I could not see much. It was very dark outside. We were probably on the interstate.

I looked up from my seat to ask Mom, "May I please lay my seat back?" She said I could, so I laid back. I too was soon asleep, and probably slept for hours. When I woke up, it was bright daylight.

The bus driver stopped at a bus station and said, "This station serves hot breakfast to go, and we will be departing in thirty minutes."

The majority of the people got off the bus. The breakfast line was extremely long. I could see the bus from where we were standing, and I prayed that it was not thirty minutes yet. I didn't want the bus to leave without us. Harold ordered a breakfast sandwich and orange juice for us, and then we headed back to the bus.

We rode for a long time. Finally, the bus driver announced, "We will be arriving in Bradenton, Florida in about ten minutes. Please make sure you take all your belongings with you and thank you for choosing Greyhound."

The bus drove up to the small bus station, and I stood up before the bus made a complete stop. I looked for Bob. Several people were standing outside the bus station and there in the crowd, I spotted Bob. No words could express the joy I felt when I spotted my big brother. I could not wait to talk to him. Mom introduced him to Harold. They loaded our luggage in the trunk of his car.

Bob seemed happy to see us. He patted me on the head, smiled and said, "You've grown." I smiled, bubbling over on the inside because I had so much I wanted to say to him. I sensed that it was not a good time to say much.

However I did say, "Bob, I missed you so very much!"

He replied, smiling, "I missed you too very much."

We all got into his car. Our first stop was a 7-Eleven. They sold gas, snacks, and limited on-the-go items.

Bob told Curtis and me to get two things each. I chose a small bag of Dorito chips and a can of orange soda pop. We placed it on the counter for him to purchase. I had my own bag. It was more than just a snack to me because Bob had bought it for me. It was a gift from Bob to me, a gift of his love for me.

I couldn't help but notice that something was different about Bob. He was much thinner and walked with a slight limp. I was concerned about him. I wondered if he was sick. I wanted to ask him what had happened, but I didn't feel like it was the right time to ask him.

When we settled in the car, I admired Mom and Bob's conversation on our way to the motel. She was giving him updates on South Carolina. From their conversation, Mom sounded like she had enjoyed South Carolina. They talked about my grandma, uncles, aunts, cousins, and Terry. I understood that Bob knew we had another brother because he spoke like he knew him. Mom spoke well about South Carolina. I wondered why she was moving us back to Florida if she enjoyed South Carolina so much. I know Mom had her reasons. Maybe she missed Bob, or she wanted to start a new life with Harold.

I asked myself those questions, and I also wondered what a motel was. I had never heard of one. So many questions were bottled up in me. I learned to be silent with Mom. She seemed so happy, and I didn't want to agitate her. I loved seeing Mom happy, so I didn't ask her any questions.

We finally arrived at the motel. Wow! The motel was a long building with a lot of doors that had numbers on them. I noticed a pool that was surrounded by families. They looked like they were having a great time. I didn't know how to swim, but I surely wanted to go over there.

Mom, Bob, and Harold got out of the car and went into an area that said "Office." Curtis and I waited in the car as ordered and just gazed at the pool area. When they returned to the car, Bob drove and parked in front of one of the doors with numbers on it. That was our room. Bob helped unload the car. Curtis, Mom, and Harold went into the room. I tagged along with Bob as he unloaded his trunk. When we were walking back to the room, Bob continued to limp.

My concern and curiosity caused the question to tumble out of me unbidden. I asked him, "What happened to your leg?"

He replied, very calmly with a simple smile, "I'm okay, I hurt it on some stairs, but I'm fine now—okay." I believe that he didn't want me to worry, but He didn't *look* or *walk* like he was fine.

When everything was unloaded from the car, Bob sat to visit with Mom and Harold. While he was sitting, I couldn't help but notice a thick scar on the outside of his ankle. Bob had tried to convince me that he was fine, so I didn't say another word about it. Later that evening, I wanted to ask Mom about the scar on Bob's ankle, but I couldn't build up enough nerve to ask.

A couple of days passed and we were preparing to leave the motel. It was nice there. When we drove away, I took away lovely memories to hold. Each morning we had gone to a small kitchenette area near the office for our morning treat. Mom called it breakfast, but it satisfied *me* as a treat.

I had eaten delicious glazed donuts that melted in my mouth and drank delicious thirst-quenching orange juice. Each night I slept in a big bed with fluffy, nice comfortable bedding. I felt like a princess. Curtis slept on a small couch that pulled out into a little bed. The bed was the perfect size for him. He seemed like he enjoyed his bed as much as I enjoyed mine.

We mainly watched western shows on television because that was Harold's favorite. It seemed like his favorite character was a man named Festus; he made Harold laugh. (It was rare to see him laugh.) Even though I think he was a happy person, he just didn't show much emotion. I could understand why Harold liked Festus. I liked him too. His character and tone of voice were very distinctive. I liked his personality and curiosity. When he talked, his eyebrows moved, unlike anyone I had ever seen. It was as if he talked with his eyebrows. He was truly one of the highlights of the western shows.

When we checked out of the motel, we stayed with Bob until they found a permanent place for us to live. Bob lived in a house called a rooming house. It was a white wooden two-story house. Several other people lived there, and they all rented their own room. The room Bob rented was on the second floor. I believe those were the stairs where Bob must have injured himself. I was very careful walking up and down the stairs. I told Curtis to be careful, and I walked very slowly up and down the stairs with him. I even prayed that we wouldn't hurt ourselves on the stairs.

Living at the rooming house was an adventure. I didn't know the people who lived there. Curtis and I were the only children in that big house. Everyone shared the same kitchen, sitting area, and bathrooms. About a week later, we were preparing to move into our own new home. The place I would soon call home was a neighborhood called Soul Ville. They were green brick duplexes. There were so many I could not count them all.

Children were playing ball in the streets. It was obvious that the neighborhood had lots of children.

We settled into our duplex. It had a kitchen, living room, and a bathroom. Bob moved in with us. He worked a lot, so I didn't see him often. The brief times he was at home he was glued to the television. We were 13 years apart, so I understand why we didn't have much in common.

Mom and Harold found jobs and Curtis and I were enrolled in school. I met a girl in my neighborhood named Kim. I noticed she didn't attend my school. I asked her what school she attended.

"I go to Wakeland Elementary, and I walk there with my brothers," she told me.

I told her that I had gone to Wakeland before our move to South Carolina, but now that we lived in the neighborhood, I would go to Samoset. Kim explained that one side of the community went to Samoset Elementary by bus, and the other side of the neighborhood walked to Wakeland Elementary.

I rushed into our duplex, ran up to Mom without any hesitation and said, "Mom! Kim attends Wakeland Elementary, my old school, and I want to go back to my old school!" No words could express how much I wanted to go back there. Samoset Elementary was the fifth school I was to attend. I was happy to see that Mom seemed concerned.

The next day she took me along with her to the School Board Administration Office and tried to get an approval letter so my brother and I could attend Wakeland Elementary. They sent us to an office where we were greeted by a man who wore a suit and tie. He looked important as he sat behind his big fancy desk.

Mom was very calm that day. She expressed to him that half of the children in our neighborhood attended Wakeland Elementary, and the other half of our neighborhood attended Samoset Elementary. She asked him if my brother and I could attend Wakeland instead of Samoset because we had attended that school before we moved to South Carolina.

He asked Mom for our address. He shuffled through some

papers, then paused for a few moments and said, "It will be best if you stay in your school zone."

I dropped my head with sadness, and then I slowly looked up and pleaded with him, "May I please go back to Wakeland?"

He looked at me, his lips tight as he shook his head no. I could not hold back the tears as they dripped from my eyes like raindrops. I remembered him saying as we walked out of his office, "One good thing about it, you don't have to walk to school in the rain."

I didn't mind if I had to walk to school in the rain, but I knew by the look in his eyes that his "no" meant "*no*." It was a final judgment, and it fell heavily upon me.

When we were on our way home Mom said to me in a calm tone, "Resa, you will meet new friends at your new school."

"Yes ma'am.," I said, my heart filled with hurt. But I realized that Mom had tried, and the final decision was out of her control. I went to Samoset with a broken heart. I felt like I didn't fit in with my peers. At that point in my life, I felt overwhelmed by so many life changes. As a result, I isolated myself at school.

The teachers seemed caring, but I don't remember having any close friends besides the few kids from my neighborhood.

The school bus ride was chaotic the majority of the time. I was terrified of my bus driver, Ms. Trumen. She didn't seem to enjoy driving the bus. She always had a mean stare as she watched us through her large rear view mirror. She seemed like she had her eyes on us most of the time while she drove the bus, but Ms. Trumen never swerved off the road. She yelled at us constantly.

Her favorite line was, "Y'all act like a bunch of hoodlums!"

I didn't know what that meant, but by the tone of her voice, it was not a compliment.

Even though my time at school was not the greatest and the bus ride home was hectic, evening time was the worst for me. The place I called home was changing. Curtis and I arrived home before Mom, Bob, and Harold. I was responsible for caring for

Curtis and cleaning the house after school.

When Mom got home from work, she prepared dinner and sipped on her alcohol throughout the evening. When dinner was cooked Curtis and I ate together at the kitchen table. Mom and Harold ate at random times. Harold usually ate in their bedroom, and Mom ate sitting on the couch in the living room, sipping on her alcohol. As the evening progressed Mom's speech slurred more and more. Her attitude became more and more aggressive. It was obvious that Mom was drunk.

I didn't understand why Mom drank so much alcohol every day. I loved her, and I was sad to see her that way. I prayed often. My prayer was, "God, please help my Mom to stop drinking and let her know that she is hurting me."

I did everything that she told me to do to the best of my ability. My daily chores were to wash the dishes and to sweep and mop the house. I then cleaned the bathroom, which included scrubbing the sink and bathtub. The bathtub often had a stubborn ring around it after everyone bathed. I cleaned with Ajax cleanser and ammonia. The products mixed together produced a horrible smell. The fumes were so powerful at times that it burned my eyes, and I could barely catch my breath. I thought the more of it I used, the cleaner the area would look. My goal was to make Mom proud of me. Unfortunately, each evening when the alcohol got the best of her, she found reasons to hit me with her violent, angry hands. It seemed that Mom hit me when she caught me looking at her or if the chores were not done to her expectation. I looked at her because I couldn't help it. I craved a mother-daughter connection with her—like some of my friends had with their moms.

Curtis was not hit as often by Mom's angry hands. But there was one evening when Mom swung at him with her fist and hit him in the mouth so hard that she split his lower lip. He cried so loudly; he sounded like he was screaming I knew he must have been in a lot of pain. His lip bled so much. I was scared, and I prayed that the bleeding would stop. Mom seemed nervous. She pampered his wound, frantically trying to stop the bleeding. After the bleeding finally stopped, we went to bed. I tried to comfort Curtis when Mom was not looking. He cried himself to sleep that night.

When we woke up the next morning, his lip was very swollen. He didn't look good. His eyes were swollen from crying so much the night before. I was afraid because usually the bruises we received were hidden under our clothes. I wondered how we were going to hide my brother's lip.

When Mom saw him that morning, she looked frightened. She said to my brother, "If anyone asks you what happened to your lip, tell them that your sister did it."

He nodded his head and said, "Yes ma'am."

She turned to me and said, "Did you hear what I said Resa?"

Very calmly, with voice trembling, I answered, "Yes ma'am." I didn't want to see my Mom in any trouble. I geared myself up for the day ahead of me.

My brother and I went to the bus stop that morning. Many of the children asked him, "What happened to his lip?"

He said exactly what Mom told him to say. Even though he seemed like he didn't want to say it, he answered, "My sister did it. She punched me in my lip."

The word spread quickly on the school bus and at school. That answer started an uproar. My peers were angry at me. I felt helpless, but I realized that it was safer for Mom if I took the blame. No one truthfully knew what went on *behind the walls I called home.*

My faith in God helped me to start each day as a new day. Even though each day ended the same, I was able to endure because God gave me peace that surpassed my understanding. I felt as if God wiped my tears away each night.

Summertime finally arrived. In spite of what went on behind the walls I called home, I had great fun with the kids in our neighborhood during the day. There were a lot of us, and we got along fairly well, just being kids. Most of the adults in my neighborhood worked during the day, including Mom, Harold, and Bob.

I didn't see Bob often, and I'm not sure if he knew what went on behind the walls I called home. The majority of the children, including Curtis and me, had the freedom to roam the neighborhood. We were a very adventurous group. We played many outdoor games. The most popular games were hopscotch, kickball, and hide-and-go-seek.

We also enjoyed building our own clubhouse. That was always a work of art. There was a huge trash dumpster on the outskirts of our neighborhood. It was a treasure chest filled with scraps of wood and left-over materials that were dumped there from the duplexes they were building near us. We collected piles from that dumpster. The trash dumped there was truly our treasures. The clubhouses that we built were similar to tree houses, but they sat on the ground. We never used hammers or nails. We propped the boards up against each other, and they miraculously stood firm, at least while we were in them.

There was a park a couple of miles down the road that served free lunches at noon. We all gathered together and walked to the park. They served each child a sandwich, fruit, milk, and juice. The rule was that we had to eat the lunch there. I enjoyed it. I felt like we had a picnic in the park each weekday. I thank God for the caring people that fed us. On Wednesdays after our journey from lunch, there was a lady by the name of Ms. Diane, who drove a small station wagon. Ms. Diane walked through our neighborhood with a big blue children's Bible in her hand. She rounded up all the children that wanted to hear a Bible story. I joined in without any hesitation.

After she had gathered us together, she took a large colorful blanket out of her car and spread it on the lawn in the middle of our neighborhood. There were as many as ten to fifteen children who sat gathered around her on the beautiful blanket. She read to us with great enthusiasm. I felt like I was there in each story. I will never forget her glowing smile, calm voice, and caring personality. She was a great example of God's love towards us, and I thank God for her.

I looked forward to Sunday mornings, as much as I looked forward to Ms. Diane on Wednesdays. Each Sunday morning a long yellow bus like a school bus with "Trinity Baptist Church" written on the side of it came through our neighborhood. They drove very slowly picking up children, including Curtis and me. Some children went on the bus without shoes on their feet. I never saw them turn a child away. We all were greeted with open arms. The bus ride was long and exciting and full of children of all various nationalities and ages. We sang songs the whole trip to church and back home. My favorite songs were "This Little Light of Mine," "He's Got the Whole World in His Hands," and "Jesus Loves Me." Those songs were so refreshing.

When we arrived at the church we entered a nice area just for kids. I had so much fun there. We sang songs; we were taught the word of God, and we played trivia games at the end. I loved it.

Before they bused us back home, they gave us a sweet filling snack. One Sunday after church they took all of us to Dairy Queen for ice cream. That was a very special day. Every time I see a Dairy Queen, I think of Trinity Baptist Church. God showed me love through so many caring people at that church. I knew God loved me in spite of the life I faced *behind the walls I called home*. I enjoyed my life outside those walls.

I did my chores before Mom got home from work and braced myself for the hectic evening ahead. Mom continued to drink alcohol obsessively. My nights were dark, but joy came in the morning when I went out on my adventures. I enjoyed my neighborhood friends and experienced the love of God through them and others.

Doretha Brown-Simmons

"God has not promised sun without rain, joy without sorrow, peace without pain. But God has promised strength for the day, rest for the labor, light for the way, grace for the trials, help from above, unfailing sympathy, undying love."

~ Annie Johnson Flint

7

OFF TO YET ANOTHER PLACE

My faith in God and connection to Him helped me to start each day as a new one. Even though each day ended the same, I was able to endure. God gave me peace that surpassed my understanding. I felt like He wiped my tears away each night.

When I was twelve years old, I started sixth grade, which was considered middle school. I attended Bradenton Middle School. A week after starting we moved into another duplex apartment that was a couple of miles from Soul Ville. The one we rented was bigger and had three bedrooms. I was so pleased to finally have my own room, and I was thrilled to start middle school. It was amazing to see many of my friends from Able Elementary, Wakeland Elementary, and those from my previous neighborhood all at the same school. God had answered my prayers again. I was able to see my old friends again.

I walked to and from school; it was a little less than two miles. Anyone that lived two miles or more from their school rode the bus. I was happy to walk. Middle school was a whole new world. I enjoyed it. I liked that I had six different classes a day. All of my classes were great.

My favorite class was sixth period, Mr. Stanley's math class. I loved the way he taught math. His enthusiasm as a teacher made learning fun. There was never a dull moment in his class. He had zero tolerance for students that didn't have an interest in learning, and he had a great passion for the students that wanted to succeed. I was determined to do my best in school. I fitted in well, and it was a safe place to me. The teachers had great interactions with the students and the majority of the students bonded well with each other. There were a couple of class clowns, but overall my sixth-grade year at Bradenton Middle School felt like one big happy family.

During my sixth-grade year, Bob did some special things with Curtis and me. He took us to the county fair and the beach. Those were places I had never gone before. The moment I entered the gates of the Manatee County Fair, I was so excited! Joy bubbled up within me and made me feel like I had entered the gates of Disney World. I had never gone there, but I was told when you entered their gates it is an amazing feeling. The county fair was my Disney World, and Bob was my hero. He took time out of his busy schedule and away from his friends to make a dream come true for Curtis and me.

We had such a wonderful time at the fair. There was so much to see and do. The live music was vibrant. I could not help but have a little dance in my step as I walked. There was food galore and lots of games to play. At each game station, someone talked through a microphone. They said things to lure people over to the games—and it worked. I won a cute little-stuffed animal after bursting a balloon with a dart. I rejoiced like the people did on the show called "The Price Is Right" when they won a new car or something of great value.

After playing a few games, we went to see the animals and then rides followed. There were lots, and lots of both. It was fascinating to see goats, rabbits, cows, and llamas face to face. The rides there were awesome. Curtis went on every ride that I went on, without any hesitation. Bob stood and watched us, with a glowing smile on his face.

On each ride Curtis and I braced ourselves for the adventure as we buckled ourselves in with nervous giggles of excitement. We shouted with great enthusiasm along with others on the ride saying, "I want to go faster!" We screamed and laughed at the same time when the ride went faster. The thrill I felt on each ride was priceless.

After the rides, Bob bought us a bag of cotton candy and a candied apple. The cotton candy melted in my mouth. It was so sweet and delicious. The candied apple looked so lip-smacking good. It had a perfect red shine. It looked too perfect to eat, but I couldn't resist. I peeled the clear wrapper off, and I licked and licked, the more I did, the sweeter it tasted. I finally took a bite, and it was so yummy. Candied apples should be shaped like shiny red hearts because every bite makes the heart smile. I thank God for that very special day at the fair.

Bob took Curtis and me to beautiful Coquina Beach several times that year. Each time we went, I was so excited. Bob usually grilled hotdogs, and we ate them with potato chips and fruit punch. He allowed us to go into the ocean. He usually stood back and observed, like a lifeguard. He knew I loved the water, but I was not good at swimming.

I felt like we had Bob's undivided attention. We showed him the beautiful shells we found, and he always showed interest in them. When we called out to him and showed him tricks that we could do in the water, he seemed amused. My favorite trick was to pinch my nose with my two fingers and put my head under water. Each time I did it, I felt like I became that much closer to becoming a better swimmer. I was so fascinated watching Curtis swim like a dolphin. I seized every moment at the beach—the sound of the waves as they rolled onto the shore, the texture of the wet sand between my toes, and most of all the priceless time with my two brothers.

Behind the walls I called home everything stayed the same. Mom continued to drink alcohol after work, and evenings continued to be the worst time for me. She continued to hit me with her violent, angry hands and became more hostile at saying hurtful things to me.

One of her most common lines was, "You are so stupid!" She compared me to my two cousins in South Carolina.

She often said, "Your cousins are so much smarter than you!" Mom seemed to enjoy saying that to me.

There was a quote I had heard since kindergarten, "Sticks and stones may break my bones, but words will never hurt me." But those types of words *did* hurt me. Even though I knew that was not how God saw me, my heart still ached to hear Mom say those words to me. I continued to pray for Mom because I envisioned her healed from alcoholism. Mom was so beautiful on the outside, and I knew God could make her just as beautiful on the inside. She was tall and slim. Her skin tone was a stunning light brown color. Her hair was black and long. She had a smile that could brighten up a room, but I rarely saw that smile.

I realized through the onset of puberty that I was growing up. That was a new stage in my life, and I was too scared to share any moment of it with Mom. I was forced to be silent within the walls I called home. I learned and talked about puberty through conversations with my friends at school and from my Health Educational Class. I thank God for the avenues He used to educate me in what I needed to know about puberty.

I wondered if Mom loved me because I had never heard her say it. She did surprise me for Christmas that year. I received a beautiful black and white ten-speed bicycle. That was my very first new bike. I cherished it along with my new handheld radio. I felt loved by her at that moment. I looked forward to going back to school after Christmas vacation. I was ready to ride my new bike to school. Bike riders left school five minutes before everyone else. That rule was probably for safety reasons, but I considered it a privilege and loved it.

March of that year I turned thirteen years old. I was officially a teenager. At that age self-image was important. I tried to be nice, look nice, and be liked by others. I was blessed to have several friends whom I trusted, and my grades in school were good. My wardrobe was slightly awkward. I wore Mom's clothes most of the time because I had very few school outfits of my own. Her clothes were too big for me, but she wanted me to wear larger clothes anyway. When I wore something that wasn't loose fitting, she ordered me to take it off. I didn't understand why and I wasn't allowed to ask. I was always considered tall for my age, and I was very thin. People often commented that I was "too skinny." I prayed that God would help me to gain weight. But I was the perfect size for basketball. I tried out for my school basketball team. I made the team and played basketball and volleyball, and enjoyed both. Our class split up into a red team and a blue team, and we played against each other.

Summertime arrived. My favorite place was the pool. It was located near the park that served free lunches. I looked forward to the free lunch in the park and going into the pool afterward. That summer was the first time I ever went into a pool, and I defiantly didn't dive in head first. I had stayed at a motel several summers before. That was the first time I ever saw a pool up close. I wanted to go into it or just touch the water, but I didn't get the opportunity.

At the age of thirteen, I finally got my opportunity. I hesitated about going into the pool because I was not a good swimmer. The first few times I went, I sat on the edge with my lower legs and feet in the water. I enjoyed every minute as I observed my peers swimming and diving off the diving board. On the third day, I finally eased my way down the steps into the pool. I went under water. I noticed it was not salt water like the water at the beach. I learned that pool water usually had chlorine in it instead of salt. That interested me. The pool was three feet deep on one end and probably ten feet deep on the other end where the diving board was located. I stayed in the three-feet-deep area because I could only swim with my head under water. I don't know if that was considered swimming, but to me it was.

It was nice. I was able to stand up each time I needed to take a breath. I tried, and I tried, but was not able to swim with my head above water. It was like my bones were made of brick because I always sank when I tried it. I felt safe in the pool because a lifeguard was there at all times. His name was Felix. He was the only adult at the pool. He was nice, but strict when it came to obeying the pool rules. It was clear that if anyone broke the rules, they were suspended from the pool area. I rarely saw my peers break the pool rules because that was the only safe place for teens to hang out, on the east side of Bradenton where I lived. It was the perfect place to be on those beaming, blazing hot summer days.

I lived in an area that was surrounded by drug addicts, drug dealers, and cars with music so loud it vibrated our windows when they passed by our home. Seeing drug transactions was second nature. Rock cocaine and marijuana were the popular street drugs.

People smoked marijuana like cigarettes. It had a very strong scent. I tried to hold my breath when I passed by people that smoked it.

A man approached me when I was on my way home from the pool one day and showed me about five little chunks of what they called rock cocaine. He offered me one, and I said, "No! I don't want that!"

He went his separate way. I felt God had protected me at that moment. I saw how alcohol had affected my Mom and how drug addicts looked so defeated, walking the streets in search of their next drug fix. I didn't want any part of that. I promised myself that I would never drink alcohol or use drugs.

I had one more year in middle school and was looking forward to high school. My eighth-grade year was very similar to seventh grade. I played basketball and volleyball. I worked as hard as I could in school because I didn't want to repeat a grade level again. That had hurt me too much. At the end of my eighth grade year, I was fifteen years old. My school had an end of the year party for the eighth-grade class.

I was surprised that Mom bought me a dress for the dance. It was a long, pink, beautiful lacy dress. She also bought me new white shoes. I felt as beautiful as all the other girls at the dance. I had a wonderful time with my friends that night. My dress was more than just a dress. I considered it a token from Mom. I still have that lacy pink dress to this very day.

I was enrolled in a summer program that prepared me for a summer job. It was a course that taught work ethics. After the course was completed, I received my certificate to work. They found me a job and gave me a city bus pass to ride to and from work. I considered that a blessing. I worked at the West Bradenton Girls Club. I loved my job. Interacting with the girls, and being a positive role model for them was so rewarding. I had always wanted to be a Girl Scout or attend a girls' club. God fulfilled my desire in a special way. I was paid to be there, and I enjoyed every moment there. I worked with girls as young as six years old, and up to fourteen years old.

The adult staff there were phenomenal at their jobs. I learned from them as well. Working there helped shape and mold my character in such a positive way. The Girls' Club promoted health, fitness, decision-making, problem-solving, and peaceful conflict resolution. There was never a dull moment there. They had so much to do, learn, and explore.

I worked Monday through Friday, five hours a day. I earned minimum wage which was $4.25 an hour. My income after taxes totaled $200.00 every two weeks. I felt so privileged to earn a paycheck doing something I enjoyed.

I gave Mom half of my earnings, per her request, to help with bills. I saved $50.00 every two weeks because my long-term goal was to buy a car. Mom didn't drive. I knew if I drove I'd be able to help drive her places. I'd also have transportation to work and school. The remaining $50.00 was used for school clothes and school supplies. I earned a total of $1000.00 that summer; $250.00 of it was saved towards a car.

Summer break was coming to a halt. It was a bittersweet time in my life. I was excited to be starting high school, but I was sad to see my summer job come to an end. It was hard to say goodbye to everyone that I had looked forward to seeing each day at work.

My first day of high school finally arrived. I remember it as if it was yesterday. I was nervous and excited at the same time. There were so many students. The freshmen stood out like a sore thumb. Most of us had the same type of lost look on our faces as we journeyed through the hallways, trying to find our classrooms. It was very different than middle school. Yes, I had gone to many different schools in my lifetime, but nothing compared to this whole new environment. The campus was much bigger, with many new faces, and the class sizes were much larger.

It was interesting how in eighth grade we were top of the class and as a ninth grader, I felt like I was now at the bottom of the barrel. The seniors stood out with stamina and pride. I could imagine how proud they were to finally be a senior in high school. The athletes stood out as well. The football players looked like real football players, and the basketball players looked like real basketball players.

After a month in school, I felt more adjusted to my high school routine. I envisioned myself persevering and succeeding. The teachers were enthusiastic and eager to teach. It was interesting to see that a lot of them were both coaches and teachers. Many of them inspired me in their own special way. One, in particular, was Coach Tschappat. I met him in eighth grade when he visited my middle school and spoke to us about highlights of high school life.

I remembered him saying, "If you study, do your best, and don't give up. You'll succeed in high school." He also said, "We, the staff, at Southeast High School, care about our students."

I was blessed to have him as a teacher in my ninth grade year. Even to this very day, I feel like he believed in me more than I believed in myself. Yes, I envisioned myself persevering and succeeding. He had faith in me and saw further into my future than I did. I strived to become the person he saw me as. I identify him as one of the angels God put in my life. He didn't know the life I faced behind the walls I called home, but he gave me the motivation to persevere as a high school student. He looked me in the face many times and said, "Doretha, you can do it. I believe in you."

Those words gave me the energy to thrive. I was blessed to be surrounded by a circle of teachers like him.

Mr. Reed was another special person—an angel to me. He was my chorus teacher. My class was called The Girls Glee Chorus. That name was truly the perfect title. The class was full of joy, cheer, and harmony. Mr. Reed was a very peaceful and calm teacher. I believe he was a Christian. I do not remember him saying he was, but he didn't need to. It was obvious. The peacefulness in him radiated throughout the atmosphere of the chorus room. I looked forward to entering his room because of the positive energy he generated into each student. Girls who were considered bullies on campus were as humble as lambs in his presence. Every song we sang felt like healing to my soul. I was honored to have a seat.

I longed to play for my high school basketball and volleyball teams. I was not able to try out for any after school activities or sports though because I needed to work to help my family. I started working after school in the Desoto Square Mall. I was a salesperson in a store called *Things Remembered*, a very nice store that sold gifts for special occasions. I enjoyed interacting with my customers and helping them decide what the perfect gift was for that special person. They had the privilege to have their gifts personalized by engraving the name or a special message on the gift.

The engraving part was done very carefully with the engraving machine. I used my hands to guide the machine as I traced the designs, names, numbers, and/or messages on the item. It was rewarding to see the smile on their faces when they saw the work of my hands on the personalized gift they had purchased. I also made duplicate keys. My job made me feel so creative.

I watched so many families as they traveled throughout the mall. Many of them seem like they enjoyed each other as a family. I often prayed that one day I would be blessed with a family of my own, and would be able to show them the love I had longed for and had so desired.

A man named Mark, who was 26 years old, worked in the clothing store across from me. He was married and had a son. Each time he talked to me, the brief conversation was always about his wife and son. It was obvious that he had an abundance of love for his family. I know God smiled on him. Mark wanted the world to know how blessed he was. Mark's family reminded me of Uncle Henry, Auntie Lenora, and Terry. Both families seemed to have so much love in them. A couple of my peers at the school described their families as close-knit. I imagined their home must have felt like safe havens.

Mom and Harold were still together, but I didn't understand the type of bond they had. He usually kept to himself. I didn't know much about him. I considered him to be calm and quiet. I know he had served in the Vietnam War. Maybe that had something to do with his demeanor.

I heard him say to Mom, "I saw a lot in the war." I never heard him say more than those few words about it or anything else. I am blessed to say that I didn't fear him, and he never violated me or harmed me in any way.

Everyone in the walls I called home worked except Curtis. He was thirteen and in school; he was too young to work. He had a teacher that he was very close to, who passed away suddenly in a tragic car accident. Curtis seemed to lose interest in school after that.

I was sad to see him grieve for so long. He shied away from his studies. I tried to comfort him and encouraged him not to give up. I tried to set a good example for him by doing my best in school.

I was determined to graduate. I planned to attend summer school and juggle it with work. My prayers and goal were to graduate early and own my own car. I knew there were steps I had to take to accomplish my goals. I studied and passed the written test. I was overjoyed to receive my learner's permit.

I worked extra hours to pay for private driving lessons. I eventually took the road test and passed it the second time. The first test went okay until I had to parallel park and tipped over one of the orange cones and didn't pass the test. The second time I was excited when she told me I passed. I wanted to hug her!

By tenth-grade, I had saved $2,000 for a down payment on a car, at a Buy Here Pay Here car dealership. In 1989 at the age of 16, I bought a yellow, four-door, 1980 Ford Fairmont. My monthly payments were approximately $200.00 a month. My faith in God was so rewarding. No words could have expressed the joy I had as I drove to school and work. I was able to help take Mom places she needed to go. She carpooled to work with a group of her coworkers most of the time. I felt blessed to help her in this little way—to provide a convenience she had not had before: transportation from her door to where she needed to go without unnecessary waiting.

I was blessed to get a job close to home. I loved working at the mall, but several of my friends worked at a nursing home near my house. I applied for a position in the dietary department, waiting tables to serve senior citizens. I was hired the day Mrs. Jewel; the supervisor interviewed me. I gave God the praise when I received the position.

I was amazed to see senior citizens in their 80's, and 90's, and one lady who was 101 years old. She had snow white beautiful curly hair. She dragged her cane when she walked to the dining room and to play bingo. They were so full of life and personality. They kept me smiling.

The summer of 1989 was adventurous; I was 17 years old, completed my tenth-grade year. I looked forward to working and going to summer school as usual. I needed to take an elective to stay on track with my plan to graduate early. I wanted to do something exciting. I chose basic swimming class. Wow! I didn't realize what I had signed up for. I imagined the class full of students with *my* basic swimming skills.

The first day of class was questionable. The instructor lectured about pool and water safety. I thought I was aware of those rules. I went to my local pool at the age of 14 and was taught pool rules.

Her lecture was on a whole other level. It started out basic and then transitioned to a lecture fit for an Olympic swimmer. Then, she toned it down when she showed a video on the importance of knowing how to float face down and on your back. The video was interesting and sounded simple, but I had a gut feeling I signed up for something bigger than I was aware of. The next day confirmed my gut feeling. We all dressed for our session in the pool. The first technique was easy. We stretched in the three foot area of the pool and then we floated face down. I was able to do it. Then she told us to float on our backs. Everyone did it with ease except for me. No matter how calm or relaxed I was, I could not stay afloat. I was embarrassed.

My instructor tried to help me, as my peers were entertained by my actions; I laid on my back as my instructor braced me up with both hands. When she removed her hands, I sunk as if my bones were made of cement. After she had tried to help me stay afloat five times, she stopped and said, "Keep trying."

The class moved on to the next step. Each student was instructed, one at a time to swim a short distance and back. They all did it with their heads above water.

I thought to myself; *I don't know what I am going to do.* I was not on the same swimming level as my peers. I wanted to become a better swimmer. To do it I could not give up or quit.

On the third day, I arrived early to meet with my instructor Ms. Smith. I expressed my concerns to her. I said, "I thought the class was for students like me. I can't float on my back or swim with my head above water yet. But I'll try my best to learn the skills needed to pass the course."

Ms. Smith was willing to work with me. She saw my determination and didn't give up on me. Ms. Smith deserved a gold medal for her patience. I didn't swim like a dolphin by the end of the course. I faced reality. I was not a good swimmer. I held my head up regardless and by the grace of God I passed the class.

I thank God my work environment was great. Behind the walls I called home, life continued as usual. I continued to pray for Mom. I realized alcohol was taking a toll on her. She didn't look healthy. However, she forced her way to work. Each evening she prepared a hot meal for us. I believe God gave her the strength and I am grateful He did. I longed for a real, deep relationship with her and I ached to see her in such bondage. I held on to faith and believed she would not be that way always. I envisioned her healed and happy. I missed Bob. I didn't see him often because of our different schedules. The brief times I did see him, I valued with all my heart.

When summer break ended, I started eleventh grade. During my second week, I was called to the office. I was nervous and had no clue why anyone at the office wanted to talk with me. My grades were good, and I stayed away from trouble. I prayed it was not a family emergency.

I walked into the office with a blank look on my face. I said to Mrs. Cummings, "I was called to the office."

She told me to have a seat. I sat twirling my fingers. A few moments passed, it felt as if it were hours. Mrs. Cummings said, "Doretha, Coach Tshappet, wants to see you."

I went to his office and was greeted with his smiling face. I nervously returned the smile.

He said, "Doretha, I reviewed your credits, you are eligible to be a senior this year."

I was speechless as tears of joy filled my eyes. No words could express the joy that bubbled within my soul as I ingested the news.

He said, "Congratulations you did it, I knew you could."

I said, "Thank you." The joy on his face made it obvious he was proud of me. He informed me of my senior privileges and the senior meetings I needed to attend.

I walked out of his office so proud of myself. I thanked God; He had blessed me with the endurance to persevere. The long nights I stayed up to study after work and the sacrificed summer vacations to attend summer school had paid off.

No matter what went on behind the walls I called home; I had stayed strong. I did not let it confine me or deprive me of a better future. I continued to remind myself of how God saw me. His word says, *"I know the plans I have for you, declares the LORD, plans to prosper you and not to harm you, plans to give you a hope and a future"* (Jeremiah 29:11 NIV).

I enjoyed senior year. The seniors accepted me. My friends in eleventh grade were happy for me. I was blessed to be connected to a positive group of peers. I soon realized I was not alone in the type of life I faced behind the walls I called home. There were others that faced obstacles similar to mine. We bonded together, encouraged each other, and triumphed through the trials.

After I had worked in dietary for six months, Mr. John, the Supervisor over the resident assistant department approached me and asked," Doretha, would you be interested in working as a resident assistant?"

I said yes without hesitation. Within a week, I was a resident assistant. I worked from 4 PM to 11 PM, five days a week. I loved the position.

I assisted the residents with their essential daily tasks. Many didn't need assistance. For the ones who did, I helped them bathe, groom, and dress. I also made sure they took their medications on time. The first thing I did when I arrived to work was review reports from the resident assistant on shift. Next I made sure everyone was in the dining room for dinner at 5:30. After the residents had dinner, they had activities such as bingo, cards and chess, or singing around the piano. The first Friday of the month was ballroom dancing at 7 PM. The residents all dressed up because it was a special occasion. The atmosphere was festive. I was amazed to see many of them danced with pizazz. The residents were from all walks of life, doctors, lawyers, nurses, teachers, farmers, factory workers, and homemakers. I realized we are all on this earth for a purpose. They inspired me to fulfill *my* purpose.

They shared their life stories. I learned so much. They told of their joys and trials of life. I summed it up as: no matter what life brings, do not give up, and hard work pays off.

It was emotionally fulfilling to see them smile or hear them say "thank you," when I did the simplest things. For example, I helped Mrs. Olive with her makeup on Fridays for the ballroom dance. She smiled and held my hand when she said, "Thank you, dear."

Ms. Vivian walked from the dining room with her walker as she juggled a hand full of goodies. I sprinted down the hall to ask, "May I help carry your goodies for you, Ms. Vivian?"

"Thank you, sweetie," she would always say with a sigh of relief. We walked to her room, and she told me stories of years ago. She had loved to bake.

Mr. Richard liked to wear baseball caps. They were usually not adjusted to fit his head. I often adjusted the back of the cap, so it would not repeatedly slide down his face while he watched television.

He said, "Thank you. I thought there was something wrong with this cap, this is much better."

"You're welcome Mr. Richard."

I watched him as he enjoyed the game without continually

lifting his cap off his face. Every person in the retirement home had a unique or special way to put a smile on my face and in my heart.

Spring break arrived. During the break, I did some soul-searching. My original goal was to complete 11th grade, then attend another summer school session to graduate early. I had accomplished it sooner than I expected. Just before Spring Break, I turned 18 years old. Graduation was three months away. I felt in my heart it was time to move out of the walls I called home and start a new life after graduation. I began to pray and trust God to bless me with an apartment and a roommate.

I wanted to stay in Bradenton for several reasons. First of all, I loved my hometown. Even though the neighborhood I lived in was not the best, on my adventures throughout Bradenton some areas were amazingly nice. I had been blessed with a job I enjoyed. My goal was to work there throughout college. I kept in mind that I might need to work a second job to accomplish my goals.

Another concern was for Mom; she was a priority on my list as well. I felt I needed to move a safe distance away but live close enough in case she needed me. I loved her.

I planned to attend the local college, Manatee Community College (MCC). It was 10 miles from my neighborhood, and the college had a great reputation. I looked forward to my new beginning. My long-term goal was to pursue a degree as a registered nurse. I had a deep passion to care for people and felt 100% sure God created me to be a nurse. I had so much love, hope and compassion to share. I knew the medical field would be the perfect place to spread my wings.

I was ready to face college life. From my research, the college required intense dedication. I was prepared for the task and thanked God for His word and His help. I was ready to spread my wings and fly. I was ready for my own walls to call home.

Doretha Brown-Simmons

*"I can do all things through Christ
who strengthens me."*

—Philippians 4:13 NKJV

8

HOME, HOME AT LAST

I was blessed to have several Christian friends at work and school. I began going to church towards the end of my senior year. I had a relationship with God and prayed often, and it was nice to fellowship in church with other believers. I was blessed to end my senior year connected in a church.

I remembered when I was six years old Mom took Curtis and me to church often. One Sunday when the preacher asked, "Does anyone want to be saved and ask Jesus into their heart? Come up to the front." I wanted that.

The choir began to sing in a low melody, "Come to Jesus."

The song was so beautiful, I whispered loudly to Mom, "Can I go up there. I want Jesus to save me and be in my heart!"

Mom said yes, and I rushed to the front of the church.. The preacher had on a long white robe and held a bottle of oil in his hand. He used his finger to put oil on my forehead. He bent down to my level and said to me in a soft tone, "Repeat after me."

I repeated his words: *"Jesus thank you for dying on the cross for me, forgive me of my sins. Come into my heart and give me everlasting life. Help me to be the kind of child you want me to be. In Jesus Name, Amen."*

I felt the love of God in my heart from that day forth. Yes, I faced many tests on my journey as a child, but God gave me peace.

The Bible is true. It says, *"Be strong and of good courage, do not fear nor be afraid of them; for the LORD your God, He is the one who goes with you. He will not leave you nor forsake you"* (Deuteronomy 31:6 NKJV).

During the time I started attending church as a young adult, many other exciting things were going on in my life. I was preparing for Grad Night, which was a special senior celebration at Walt Disney World. We traveled together on charter buses—a two-hour journey to Disney. My prayers, at last, were answered. I had dreamed of visiting the wonderful World of Disney for so long. When I entered the gates, it was more amazing than I had ever imagined. The place was full of joy and adventure. I had the time of my life!

After Grad Night, I prepared for my prom. Two of my classmates asked me to the prom. I didn't want to hurt one by saying yes to the other, so I went to my prom alone. I wore a beautiful royal blue, silk ruffled dress. I had my hair in a French Role, with hair accessories to match my dress. I felt like a princess. I had the opportunity to dance with both of the classmates who had invited me to the prom. I had a great time.

Graduation day finally arrived. Mom, Harold, Bob, and Curtis were there. It was one of the most honorable moments of my life.

I decided to go to the restroom before we were seated for the ceremony. A simple trip to the restroom almost caused me to miss my graduation. Because when I tried to leave the bathroom stall, the latch on the door wouldn't budge. It was jammed! I used all my might to dislodge it, but it wasn't moving a single bit. I quickly tired out due to the force I was expending and the thoughts running through my mind, *I got to get this opened! I made it this far, and I'm going to miss my own graduation!* In a panic I yelled, "Help! Help! Somebody! Help! I'm locked in here!"

Thankfully a group of my peers, who came looking for me, heard my pleas for help. When they entered the restroom, they were hysterical, telling me to pull the latch as hard as I could. They asked questions like, "How did you lock yourself in there? How are you going to get out?" To all their questions, I had no answer.

Finally, my fight-or-flight mode kicked in; I was ready to climb the walls, if need be, to get out. Suddenly, I saw my exit point: *under* the door. I wiggled my way out, to see my peers laughing themselves to tears. I had always taught myself to *look up* in life, but during this moment *looking down* was my way out.

We rushed into the auditorium. It was a beautiful sight to see my entire class of 1991, seated together wearing their white caps and gowns. The atmosphere was complelty filled with excitement, anticipation, and happiness.

When my name was called to walk across the stage, I was up on the platform in no time. I was ready to receive my diploma! As I stood smiling, my heart was overwhelmed in a good way. It teeming with success and faith. Graduating was very rewarding.

I sat in my room one day, shortly after graduation, thanking God for how far He had brought me. I noticed my yearbook lying on the shelf. I picked it up. The front cover was titled; *"Rippin', Thru The Year 1991."* I have it at my side 23 years later as I am writing this book. I opened the front page, as I did 23 years ago, and read what my friend Camaro wrote on the majority of the page. She penned, *"Doretha, it was nice knowing you these past years! We have had so many memories together and those memories I will never forget. I am happy that you were there when I needed you! Take care and keep God first in your life."* Then she wrote a quote underneath her note. The words forever strengthened my life in a positive, supernatural way. It says, *"May God enable you to turn your scars into stars, your obstacles into opportunities and your problems into possibilities."* I held onto those words from that day forward. It became my theme. To this day I use it to encourage others, including myself.

Coach Tshappet wrote on page seven, next to his picture, "Doretha, you made it! I knew from day one that you would! Best of luck in all you do! Love, Coach Tshappet."

On page 36 noted, was our class song, *"Tomorrow"* by The Winans, a powerful, heartfelt message in the words of the song. It is one of my favorites to this very day. On the same page, our Class Motto summed it up by saying, *"We do not know what the future holds but we know who holds the future."*

I knew without a shadow of doubt that God held my future.

"I have engraved you on the palms of my hands.
Your walls are always in my presence."

—Isaiah 49:16 GW

9

My Very Own Walls Called Home

I began to pack the belongings in my room with faith that I would have an apartment and a roommate before I started college. I began removing pictures and posters from my walls. I kept my two favorite pictures in place. One was a picture called, "Footprints in the Sand," a poem with the image of one set of footprints on a beach. The poem encouraged me that God was with me even through my toughest trials and tribulations. The picture shows one set of footprints in the sand were symbolic of God's footprints as He carried me through my trials. The author was noted to be unknown. I thank God for the person who wrote it. The other picture I kept on my wall was a plaque called, "One Day at a Time," the words on it were from a hymn. I stood and faced the wall with that plaque more times than I could count and whispered the song for comfort.

I was the first person in my family to attend college, and it was never mentioned behind the walls I called home. I was grateful; my close friend Maria from high school was coached by her parents on the steps needed to prepare successfully for college. Both of her parents were teachers. She knew everything about the application process and the registration guidelines. She showed me how to apply for financial aid, grants and scholarships. I thanked God for her willingness to help me.

One summer afternoon, I went to the college to turn in my financial aid forms. I noticed my classmate Patricia standing in line. She was very popular and had a great personality. We talked while we waited. The conversation came up about my plans to move into the new apartment complex called Citrus Meadows. She said, "I'm looking for an apartment."

I responded, "I'm looking for a roommate."

She answered without hesitation, "I'll be your roommate!"

At that moment I knew, beyond a shadow of a doubt, that she was the one God wanted me to choose as my roommate.

We exchanged phone numbers. I called her later that day, and we made plans to meet at the apartment office to tour the two bedroom model. The next day we not only toured the model apartment, but we filled out the lease application. We were so excited when we left the office. Our glowing smiles were as bright as the Florida sunshine.

Patricia's mother had passed away in a tragic car accident when she was eight years old. She had lived with family members throughout her life. She never complained or seemed down about her life without a mother. Her sparkling personality inspired me. Two weeks later Patricia and I received the exciting news. Our application process was completed. We were told our apartment would be ready to move into in one month. The timing was perfect because that was a week before college started.

After graduation I remained living behind the walls I called home for two more months. During that time, a pastor by the name of Pastor Raymond moved into our town from South Carolina. He was introduced to Mom and Harold. He was from the same state they were, but they did not know him until he moved to Bradenton. All three of them connected as thou they had been close friends for years.

Pastor Raymond was a tall, slender man with light brown skin. He looked to be in his early fifties. He had a peaceful countenance to him and was a great listener too. It was obvious that he was on a mission from God. He always included the word of God in his conversations. When he visited the walls I called home; I was blessed to be present during many of his visits. I sat in my room and listened to the conversations. I was stunned and amazed how Mom, along with Harold, honored and fellowshipped with him.

He invited our family to church. Even though I attended a different church, I chose to join Mom and Harold without hesitation. Bob and my younger brother did not go with us. It would have been nice to have them with us, but I was grateful to see Mom and Harold attend church.

Pastor Raymond impacted Mom, Harold and me in a powerful way. We attended church together often. The way Pastor Raymond taught from the Bible, I believe a five-year-old could have understood his sermons. It was so plain and clear. He ended each sermon leaving me hungry to hear his next message. I believed Mom and Harold felt the same way because they did not miss a Sunday. One night I arrived home from work and noticed Mom reading a book at the kitchen table. I was curious because it looked like she was reading the Bible. I went to the kitchen to get a glass of water, just to get a closer look at the book in her hand. It was the Bible. I was speechless, and my hands trembled as I reached for a glass.

She asked, "How was work?"

I responded, "Ma'am?" I had heard what she said, but it was unusual to see her reading the Bible, and I was nervous, not knowing how to begin the conversation. It was odd for her to ask me how work was and not to hear her words slur when she asked. I realized at that moment: Mom was sober.

My voice trembled as I answered her question, "Work was good." I wanted to say more, but I was speechless.

I went to my room and maneuvered around the boxes that were packed for my move. I was shocked by what I had just experienced behind the walls I called home. Even though I prayed and envisioned the day I would see Mom in that state of mind. I noticed she was calmer since she started going to church, but what I observed that night was a miracle. I knelt down by my twin bed in the corner of my room and prayed to God. I whispered, "Thank You, God." Tears rolled down my face onto my bed. I woke up the next morning on my knees.

It was a Saturday morning. I left my room to the smell of bacon. The living room was so bright; I automatically squinted my eyes. The curtains were open! The curtains were never opened, and the living room was always dark. For the very first time, I was greeted by the sunlight as it radiated throughout the house. I tiptoed through the living room. I felt surrounded by God's glory. Everything was vivid as I felt His presence.

Mom was around the corner in the kitchen cooking breakfast. She glowed as she stood at the stove. She had gospel music playing very low in the background. That was unusual, and I was astonished. I felt like I was in a dream as I stood back and admired her. It was obvious she saw life in a whole new light.

"Know therefore, stand and see this great thing which God will do before your eyes."

—1 Samuel 12:16 NKJV

10

New Kind Of Home In The Old Walls

I Called Home

Mom noticed me standing near the kitchen and said, "Good morning, Resa," with an inviting smile on her face. I felt like a shy little girl with butterflies in my stomach, because finally at the age of eighteen, she greeted me in a loving, motherly way.

I said, "Good morning." I was at a standstill not knowing what to expect next.

She said, "Come in, sit, and have breakfast with me." I eased my way into the kitchen and sat in my favorite place at the table. I didn't want to say or do anything that would upset this blessed peace. She served grits, eggs, and bacon.

I felt honored to dine at the table with my mother. I cherished each and every second. I ate slowly, savored each bite not rushing time because I had waited for a moment like this all my life. I was astonished at the transformation I saw in her as I sat trying not to stare at her. I was joyful from the inside out and speechless at the same time as we listened to the gospel music playing in the background. I did not want the moment to end, but it was time for me to get ready for work.

While excusing myself from the table, I said, "Thank you, Mom. Breakfast was delicious. I'll wash the dishes."

She said, in a calm tone as she rose from the table and gathered our dishes, "I'll wash them."

Smiling softly, I said, "Thank you," and went to get ready for work. I went into my bedroom, closed the door behind me, and then danced around the boxes as King David danced before the Lord in the Bible. It did not stop there. I went to work and could not keep the good news I had witnessed and experienced to myself.

With great enthusiasm, I said joyously to everyone I saw, "Hello! I had breakfast with my mother this morning!"

Most of the people had a puzzled look on their face, not at what I said but how I said it. After I had thought about it, I understood why. I was overexcited, and there was no way to contain my joy, no matter how hard I tried.

"Trust in the Lord and do good. Then you will live safely in the land and prosper. Take delight in the Lord, and he will give you your heart's desires. Commit everything you do to the Lord. Trust him, and he will help you." —Psalm 37:3-5 NLT

God hears and heals, no matter how complicated the situation may seem. My faith allowed me to see through spiritual eyes my mother delivered, and no matter how it looked in the natural eyes, I kept on believing God's promises.

The next day we went to church. We worshiped with songs as usual before Pastor Raymond started his sermon. I noticed tears rolling down Mom's face. I never saw her shed a tear before. By her actions and facial expression, I understood that they were tears of joy as she stretched her hands towards heaven as if surrendering herself to God. There was obviously a transformation in her. Next she sang and clapped with joy beyond anything I can explain. Obviously, she was a new creation in God, through a mighty miracle. She was able to resist the devil, and he had fled. Alcohol was no longer the spirit she depended on to drown her pain. She turned to God and the help of His Holy Spirit.

"Therefore, submit to God. Resist the devil and he will flee from you." —James 4:7 NKJV

For the first time in my life, I was able to feel safe and secure behind the walls I called home. I finally wanted to be home and wanted to be near Mom. There was so much I wanted her to know about me, and I wanted her to know I was proud of her. One evening I heard a soft knock on the door of my room. I asked in a high pitch whisper, "Who is it?" The knock was unexpected. Mom answered in an echoing tone, "It's me. May I come in?"

"Yes, Ma'am," I answered.

She entered my room and sat next to me on my bed. There was a brief pause in the room. Then she said to me in a soft tone, "I stopped drinking alcohol. God healed me, and I feel so much better. I can see life much more clearly now."

I said, "Yes, ma'am."

She then said, "I'm sorry for all I have done and said to hurt you. I'm asking you to forgive me. I asked God to forgive me."

I felt a part of my broken heart mend. I had never heard mom say those words to me. She could not hold back the tears.

I said to her, "Yes, ma'am. I forgive you." I wanted to wipe the tears away from her beautiful face as I continued to say, "I see how much you've changed, and I love what I see. I thank God you're my mother."

I believe it was a moment of inner healing for both of us. I knew God turned my scares into stars at that moment in time. And Mom's obstacles into opportunities of healing and liberation. I will always keep God first in my life and trust in Him because the reward is great.

"Now unto him that is able to do exceeding abundantly above all that we ask or think, according to the power that worketh in us,..."

—Ephesians 3:20 KJV

I was exceedingly blessed to experience some valuable time with Mom behind the walls I called home, even though the time was drawing close for moving into my own apartment. I looked forward to many future visits to the place I had once called home. I discovered that Mother was growing stronger in her relationship with God. It showed through our talks about the Bible, and her peaceful ability to have self-control in situations that once angered her.

She had an amazing sense of humor. One of her sayings was, "Holy Spirit, please hold me." She said it in a way that made it hard not to chuckle. We talked and laughed with each other. Those times were so precious. I heard a quote that said, "Laughter is the best medicine." It's true because joy-filled moments like these were healing to my soul.

"A merry heart does good, like a medicine,
but a broken spirit dries up the bone"

—Proverbs 17:22 KJV

11

MY OWN WALLS CALLED HOME

My scheduled move-in day arrived, and I was ready to begin a new chapter of life in *my own walls called home*. Patricia and I arrived at the apartment leasing office at the same time that day. We walked in together. It was obvious that the office manager was happy to see us.

"Hi! Are you two here to sign your lease and pick up your keys?" she asked in a vibrant tone.

"Yes," we replied.

She retrieved the keys and escorted us to our apartment in her golf cart. When we arrived, she pointed and said, "Yours is the one upstairs on the left." It was located on the second floor, just as we requested. We felt that it was safer living on the second level instead of the first. We were so excited.

I responded, "Yes! We're on the second level."

Patricia said, "Wow. We have one with a sliding glass door and balcony."

"I figured you two would like this one," the manager replied.

On the ride to our apartment, we noticed some of the apartments had large windows instead of a sliding glass door with a balcony. We felt that the balcony was a bonus. It was the perfect size to fit two, small outdoor chairs and a couple of small flower pots.

The manager walked upstairs with us, and she unlocked the door. We took a grand tour of the place inside the walls we would call home. We walked in, and the walls were white as snow. The carpet was a beautiful sky blue color throughout, except for the kitchen and bathroom that had white tile. The windows had white blinds on each one. The appliances in the kitchen were all white and brand new. Both bedrooms had walk-in-closets.

At the end of our walk-through, the manager asked with a glowing smile, "What do you think?"

We returned the smile and in harmony said, "I love it!" Patricia and I looked at each other and smiled, amazed at our harmony.

The three of us left the apartment, and then returned to the leasing office where we signed our lease and received our keys. I felt like I walked out of that office into a whole new beginning.

I heard in a perky low subtle tone, "Doretha, we are official roommates!" Patricia said. As if her dream became a reality that very moment, as she dangled her key up high in her hand.

I responded, "Yes, we're roommates. I thank God for making it happen."

We entered our cars and drove to our apartment to unload our boxes. On my way there, I thanked God because He truly blessed me with the desires of my heart. Patricia and I got along as if we had been close-knit friends for many years. We settled into our apartment. We had the basic necessities and most of all we had God.

After one week, the first day of college came. Patricia and I carpooled with Maria that day. We were glad we did because the college parking lot was full and it was hard to find a parking space at 8:45 AM. It seemed as if every student had a 9 AM class. We found a parking space after we drove around for ten minutes.

The college campus was three times the size of our high school campus. The task of finding my class in less than five minutes was an adventure. Thankfully, I found it. By the end of the day, I noticed that most of my instructors were addressed as "Professor" and if they had a doctorate, they were addressed as "Doctor".

My life was busy. I was a full-time student, I worked full-time, and I went to church once or twice a week. Being a Christian helped separate me from temptations that could have led me down the wrong path as a young adult. God planted His Word in the core of my heart to keep me in alignment with His truth. Patricia attended church with me on the Sundays she did not work.

Maria was a Christian as well as her siblings, mother, father and grandmother. Their family seemed to be rooted in a solid foundation in Christ. I enjoyed the times I visited her house and her grandmother's house, which was next door to their house. Both houses were large and most of all, the atmosphere felt comforting to me.

One day she said to me, "Doretha, honey, you can call me Grandmother because I feel like you are one of my grandchildren." From that day on I called her grandmother. I was honored. She was in her eighties, yet so full of youth. She was a retired teacher, and her late husband had been a preacher. I loved to listen to her talk; her words were full of wisdom. She set a great example for younger women. I admired Grandmother's peaceful spirit and conversations about her life and family. She described her husband as a righteous man. It was obvious she held onto many precious memories. She even kept his office untouched in honor of him.

I wonder if he was similar to Pastor Raymond. Pastor Raymond set a great example as a leader of God. He was calm and attentive. I never saw him angry. His personality rubbed off onto those around him, especially my church family, which included my mother, Harold and Patricia.

"My dear brothers and sisters take note of this:
everyone should be quick to listen,
slow to speak and slow to become angry."
—James 1:17 NKJV

It would have been nice if more people truly lived by the above noted scripture.

Many types of people crossed the path of my young life. I was 19 years old and realized at a young age that some were placed in my life for a reason and a season, some for a lifetime, others were with me for only a brief time. During that time, no matter how long or short, there seemed to be a reason for each individual. Some people brought joy, kindness, and respect while others brought heartaches and pain. I cherished the special people God placed in my life. I prayed that God would help me endure and forgive the ones that brought hurt into my life. No one told me life would be easy and free of trouble, but God's Word gave me peace, hope, and a sound mind through it all.

"These things I have spoken unto you, that in me ye might have peace. In the world ye shall have tribulation: but be of good cheer; I have overcome the world."
—John 16:33 KJV

I managed to remember to keep God first no matter how busy life was because there was a time I didn't attend church often. I realized that without God involved in my life, coping with daily life would be difficult. I went to church on Tuesday nights and Sunday mornings.

I was in walls I called home—my apartment—for a year. A normal week for me was school Monday through Friday from 8AM until 2PM, then work at the retirement home from 3PM to 11PM five days a week. Tuesday nights I attended Bible study. I worked extra shifts on weekends to afford my bills.

Many Sunday mornings after working the night shift until 7:30AM, my body was exhausted. I arrived home and dove into bed after setting my alarm clock to wake me up in an hour. I was tempted to press the snooze button, but instead, I prayed, "Dear God, give me the strength to press my way to church and see what I would have missed if I had stayed in bed." I got up and turned on my praise and worship music as I dressed for church. That music energized me.

Patricia, Mom, Harold and I usually carpooled. Patricia blended in as if she was part of my family. I enjoyed the family time together. Harold was a man of few words as usual, but he faithfully attended church. The church service was like the icing on the cake for all of us. It was obvious the services had a powerful impact on us because our conversations in the car were based on the church service. My day felt complete after church, and I felt ready to face another week.

Pastor Raymond approached me one night after Bible study. He said, "Sister Doretha," with his eyes squinted as if he was in deep thought.

I answered, "Yes Sir, Pastor Raymond."

He said, "I see something special in you, and I would like you to prepare a fifteen-minute message from the Bible to speak on next Tuesday night."

I was caught off guard, honored, and nervous—all at the same time, because I had never spoken in front of a group of adults before. Instantly I felt God wanted me to speak on Psalm 23.

Pastor Raymond spoke his messages and sermons as if it was second nature. It was far from second nature for me. I practiced what I was going to say over and over. I prayed, "Dear God, I thank you for the opportunity to speak to your people. I know I am a bold soldier in your army. I fear no one. I can do all things through You as You strengthen me. It is not I Lord, but your Holy Spirit in me. My desire is to do your will in my life. I pray that You would increase in me God, as I decrease. You are the potter I am the clay; continue to mold me into what you created me to become. I want to speak what You want me to say to your people." I prayed and encouraged myself. I felt His peace cover me. The next Tuesday I spoke.

Pastor Raymond called me up front. He informed everyone that I was going to speak. I knew everyone there including Mom, Patricia, and Harold. There was less than 100 of us. Some of them had curious looks on their faces and probably wondered what a 19-year-old had to say to a group that was ninety percent over the age of 35 years old.

I began by greeting the congregation with, "Hello, I thank Pastor Raymond for this opportunity to share God's word with you this evening." Then I said a brief prayer, "Dear God, my precious

Maker of heaven and earth. Thank you for sending your only begotten son Jesus Christ to pay the price for our sins, and as a result, we have an opportunity to have life and have it more abundantly. I stand as your humble servant speaking your word as it is given to your people; help me in your Holy Name Amen."

After I had prayed I asked everyone, "Please, open your Bibles to Psalm 23 and I will be reading the whole chapter."

Immediately I began reading *"The LORD is my shepherd; I shall not want. He makes me lie down in green pastures; He leads me beside the still waters. He restores my soul; He leads me in the paths of righteousness For His name's sake. Yea, though I walk through the valley of the shadow of death, I will fear no evil; For You are with me; Your rod and Your staff, they comfort me. You prepare a table before me in the presence of my enemies; You anoint my head with oil; My cup runs over. Surely goodness and mercy shall follow me all the days of my life, and I will dwell in the house of the LORD forever"* (Psalm 23 NKJV).

I summed it up and said, "God is the head of our lives, and He can supply our needs. He can restore us if we only allow it. No matter what we walk through in our lives, we should not fear evil or death because God is with us. He will comfort us. He will prepare a table before us in the presence of our enemies. He anoints us continually, and our blessings will overflow because His goodness and mercy follow us all the days of our lives."

I had spoken several times since that message before Pastor Raymond informed us he was moving back to South Carolina. He had moved here by faith in God. Lives were healed, delivered and set free. I was especially grateful for his work that had included what had happened in my mother's life.

Several times we visited a particular church with Pastor Raymond. Within my heart, I felt it was the right church for me when Pastor Raymond moved on. I prayed for direction and confirmation on which church to attend. One Saturday while I was in the mall I spotted Pastor Simon and his wife walking together. I could not help but notice that they were wearing the same colors. He was clothed in a tan-colored suit, and she was draped in a fashionable tan dress that complimented his suit. He was the pastor of the church I prayed to God about attending. This divine encounter was perfect. I was excited to see them, but at the same time I tried to keep my composure as I walked up to greet them. Reaching out my hand to shake theirs I said, "Hello, my name is Doretha. I attend Pastor Raymond's church, and he is leaving soon. We will miss him."

He responded, "Yes, he will be missed." Pastor Simon had a deep raspy voice that sounded like he was blessed with an internal vocal microphone. There was a brief pause.

I wanted to say, "My family and I enjoyed the times we visited your church with Pastor Raymond and we are searching for a new church," but before I said a word it was as if he read my thoughts.

He said, "You and your family are welcome to come to our church."

His wife (Mother Simon) smiled at me as she reached her arms out to give me a hug. She said while hugging me in the middle of the mall, "We would love to have you all join us."

That was music to my ears and an answer to my prayers. Mom, Harold, and Patricia were excited when I shared the news with them, and they joined me in Pastor Simon's church. I believed Pastor Raymond connected his members with Pastor Simon's church in advance because he knew his mission was almost completed in our town. I thank God he did. I believe he saw how we were drawn by his biblical messages, the people, and the music.

Before Pastor Raymond moved away, he said in a peaceful voice, "You are all in good hands with Pastor Simon. He is a great pastor."

I believe everything that was taking place was God's divine plan from before the beginning of time. This was a new church and a new beginning. Pastor Simon had been a pastor for over 20 years. He and his wife were about 60 years old. They were great Christian leaders in our community. I was honored to be a part of their church. I became a part of the women's ministry, and I had the chance to continue the work God started in me at Pastor

Raymond's church. I was given the opportunity to speak God's word to others and encourage them. When I saw someone give their life to Christ (be "born again"), I was overwhelmed with joy. Many times I could not hold back the tears because, to me, that is the greatest sight to see.

"If we confess our sins, He is faithful and just to forgive us our sins and to cleanse us from unrighteousness."

—1 John 1:9 NKJV

"He who believes in the Son has everlasting life..."

—John 3:36 NKJV

New Year's day of 1993, I was 20 years old. Patricia and I were talking as usual in our living room, and she said, "I want to move to Miami. Will you move there with me?"

She caught me by surprise. I said, "Patricia, is this your New Year's resolution, April fool's joke?"

She said, "No, I am not joking." Even though she had a slight smile on her face I could tell she was serious.

I asked, "Why do you want to move there?"

Filled with enthusiasm she pulled out the classified section of a newspaper ad that read, "Do you want to make three times the amount of money you are making now? If your answer is yes, this is the job for you. You have to be 18 or older, a female and want to be a model. Call the number below."

I said, "The ad does not sound good. It seems too good to be true."

She said, "If we got a job with a money offer this big we wouldn't have to work as hard as we do now. And we won't have to apply for student loans. We would have enough money to pay for college. My New Year's resolution is to work less and make more money, and this is the only opportunity without a college degree."

I said, "I don't feel right about it. So, no, I don't want to move there and be a model."

"Pray about it," she said.

I said, "That was not my New Year's resolution."

Patricia had already made up her mind, and she seemed to have high hopes that my answer would be "yes." I went to my room after our conversation. I knew Patricia would get the job because she was the picture-perfect model.

Upon her leaving I knew I wouldn't have enough money to stay in the apartment alone. I had three options: search for another roommate, move back home with my family or find a one bedroom apartment I could afford on my own. Of the three options, I most wanted my own one bedroom apartment. I prayed and the next day I searched for an apartment. The first place I went to was our apartment leasing office. The manager was there alone. I said, "Hello, Mrs. Betty how is your day?"

She said warmly, "Hello, I'm well."

I said, "My roommate has planned to move soon. I want to know how much your one bedroom apartments cost."

She pulled out a pamphlet and showed me the price. It was more than I could afford. I said, "Oh, I can't possibly afford to pay that much."

She said, "You can find another roommate and keep your current apartment."

I said, "No, ma'am, I want to try to find a one bedroom apartment I can afford."

She said, "You and Patricia will need to give me a 30-day notice when you decide to move. We will miss you both."

I agreed, and on my way out of the office, I looked back at her and said, "I will miss living here." I walked out of the office and felt hopeless for a moment; then I tried to encourage myself as I drove away from the office. I thought, *No matter how bleak my situation looks, I know God didn't bring me this far in life to abandon me now.*

"Incredible as it may seem, God wants our companionship. He wants to have us close to Him. He wants to be a father to us, to shield us, to protect us, to counsel us, and to guide our way through life."

~ Billy Graham

12

YET ANOTHER PLACE TO CALL HOME

I drove to a nearby apartment leasing office called Oakmeade Apartments. I walked into the office and was greeted by a woman behind the desk, "Hello, my name is Joanne. I'm the manager."

"Hello, my name is Doretha Brown. I want to know what your monthly rate is for a one-bedroom apartment."

"The one-bedroom apartments start at $300.00 a month for one person." My hopes skyrocketed. I thought to myself in a flash, Yes! Thank you, God. I can afford a one-bedroom.

She asked, "Where do you live? What do you do for a living?"

I said, "I live in Citrus Meadows with a roommate. I am a full-time college student, and I work full-time. My roommate told me a few days ago that she is moving to Miami. I can't afford to live there when she moves away. I am praying for a one-bedroom apartment I can afford. I know I can afford to stay in a one-bedroom here in Oakmeade."

She went on to say slowly, "I don't have any one-bedrooms available. I can put you on a waiting list." My high hopes quickly took a nosedive.

The manager said, "Write your name and telephone number on this form and I will keep it on file. If I have a one-bedroom available in the next few months, I will call you."

I said, "Thank you," and left. I decided to end my search for that day and went back to my apartment. When I entered the door, Patricia and Maria were sitting in the living room watching television. I was happy to see both of them there. We sat and talked about Patricia's New Year's resolution. She explained to us how exhausted she was trying to survive on minimum wage income and attending school full time.

I knew how exhausted she felt because I was exhausted too. It was obvious her situation took a toll on her more because she was not happy with her job as a telemarketer. I was happy as a resident assistant. The staff I worked with was a great team. Each resident had a special place in my heart, and I had learned a lot from them over the years.

Maria did not need to work. She lived with her parents. Her family wanted her to attend college and make good grades. She always made good grades. I enjoyed Maria's company. She was a good listener and gave great advice. It was obvious that Maria had a close bond with her mother and grandmother because their traits of wisdom and knowledge seemed to have rubbed off on her.

I was on winter break from college and had extra private time to soul search. I knew I needed a miracle in my life. My desire was to live in my hometown, graduate from college with a degree as a registered nurse, and then move into my own apartment and eventually marry and have children. I was blessed to be in a church home where I continued to grow as a Christian, but I felt as if I was faced with obstacles bigger than me. I came to the conclusion that I needed to fast and pray for three days. I tuned out all distractions and had some private time with God. He was my refuge all of my life, my weapon against the trials and adversity. Those three days were a sacred time in my life that I will never forget. I surrendered all of me to Him. I did not want to go back home and live behind those walls again, but if it were God's will for me, I would go.

I refused to give up on God because He never gave up on me. After three days I felt a spiritual breakthrough and my faith soared.

"But they that wait on the Lord shall renew their strength; they shall mount up with wings as eagles; they shall run, and not be weary, and they shall walk, and not faint."

—Isaiah 40:31 KJV

The next day I received a call from the manager of Oakmeade Apartments. When I answered the phone, I heard, "Hello, may I speak to Doretha Brown?"

"This is Doretha Brown speaking."

"This is Joanne, the manager of Oakmeade Apartments. Can you come to my office before five o'clock today?"

I said, "Yes, I will be there soon." After hanging up the phone, without hesitation, I grabbed my keys and purse. Then I put my shoes on faster than ever before, dashed out my door and down the stairs into my car. The only thing that slowed me down was the 25 miles per hour speed limit. While driving I kept on thinking, *Why does she want to see me? Why does she want to see me?*

I got out of my car and sprinted up to her office door. I put my hand on the doorknob, paused and took a deep breath before entering her office. I was trying to keep my composure. I went inside and before I said anything, Mrs. Joanne stood up with papers in her hand and a smile on her face.

She said, "Hello, good news. I have a one-bedroom apartment for you, and it will be ready to move into, in 45 days."

I had goosebumps. I almost lost my composure with excitement as I felt my heart fill with joy. I said, "Thank you very much, Mrs. Joanne. You are a blessing."

She smiled, handed me the papers she was holding and said, "Fill these out and return them to me soon."

"But God did listen! He paid attention to my prayer."
—Psalm 66:19 NLT

I took the leasing application home, filled it out and returned it the next day. Patricia got her job in Miami the same day I turned in my leasing application. We told our leasing office manager that we were moving in 45 days. When we went back to our apartment, I went to my room and sat on my bed. I gazed around my room. The walls were white as snow. I had a few of my favorite plaques on the wall. The primary color of my room was purple. My comforter set, lamp and sheer curtains all were purple with white blinds up to the window. The blinds and curtains were always open at the first sign of sunlight. I joyfully opened the vertical blinds at the balcony door in the living room each morning. The radiant sun that beamed through the window gave me a sense of freedom behind the walls I called home. I never wanted to live in a dark home again. To this day, I allow the rays of sunlight to radiate throughout my home in Florida.

The time arrived to move into my one-bedroom apartment. I was mesmerized when Mrs. Joanne walked me to my apartment. It was located upstairs in the building behind her office. The moment she unlocked the door, and we walked inside, I inhaled the faint smell of the freshly painted white walls. She walked me through each room. The first thing I noticed was the large window with white blinds that complemented the living room. The dining area was adjacent to the living room. It was the perfect size for my small round dining room table and four chairs. There was two entrance ways through the kitchen. I followed her down the hallway to my bedroom. It was twice the size of my bedroom in my previous apartment, and it had a walk-in closet. Then she showed me the bathroom at the end of the hallway. I was overwhelmed with the feeling of gratitude and joy as I thought to myself, "Thank you, God, for Mrs. Joanne and thank You for Your gracious love for me."

The apartment complex was built in 1974, and I moved there in 1993. I remembered walking past Oakmead Apartments ten years prior, on my way to the park to eat free lunch. Even though it was an older apartment, it was new to me.

Later the same day Harold, Bob, and Curtis moved my boxes and furniture to my apartment. I admired the three of them working together as a team to help me. Mom was at my side. She helped me unpack my boxes. Then she helped hang my light blue sheer curtains on the living room window and my sheer purple curtains on the bedroom window. I cherished our time together. We accomplished a lot in one evening. It was obvious my family was happy to help me settle into my apartment.

Before Bob left, he said, "Resa, when someone knocks on your door make sure you look through your peephole before you answer the door."

I said, "OK," as I stood and watched them walk down the stairs.

As they walked away, mom turned around and said, "Resa, always double-check your door to make sure it is locked."

"Yes ma'am, I will."

My family was obviously concerned about me living alone. I went inside my apartment and locked my door. Then I turned the doorknob, I double checked it to make sure it was locked. I made it a routine to double-check it each time I locked my door. And I always looked through the peephole before I answered a knock at the door. I was not afraid to live alone, but I wanted to be safe. I was looking forward to my new life behind the new walls I called home.

Maria visited me often. Her knock on my door had a special rhythm, but I stuck to my routine. I used the peephole before I answered. It was nice when she visited, but her primary conversation was about a young man that was living in her grandmother's home while she was away for six months. Maria constantly reminded me that he was a Christian, and he talked about the Bible all the time.

She said, "Doretha, he talks about the Bible, God, and the church more than you. He comes to our house often. Mom and Dad always greets him with open arms, and they talk for hours. When I am there, they always ask me to sit in on their conversations. I never say no because that would be rude."

I said, "If they always ask you to sit in on their conversation, maybe your parents are trying to connect you two together."

"No!" She answered with her high pitch voice, "He talks way too much." She propped her elbows on her knees and rubbed her forehead with her fingertips as if the thought of dating him gave her a headache.

I asked her, "What are you going to do?"

She said, "I don't know, but this cannot go on forever."

Maria was brilliant, and I was surprised she did not have a plan and had not talked to her parents about how she felt about the situation. A month later she came up with a plan. We were in my apartment sitting at the dining room table studying, and she popped up a question out of nowhere and asked, "Doretha, will you meet him?"

"Meet who?" I asked.

"The guy who's staying in Grandmother's house," she said.

"Oh, the guy you've been ducking and dodging."

"Yes, he has a lot of faith. He asked God in fine detail the type of wife he wanted," she replied.

"Oh really, um, I pray God gives him the wife he requested." I was trying to focus on my studies, looking in my book the whole time. I was hoping she would catch on and focus more on studying for our upcoming math test and less on the guy's future wife."

"Doretha," she cried in a high-pitched voice.

She startled me; I popped my head out of my book "What?" I asked, showing her that she had my undivided attention.

Looking me straight in the eyes she said, "The type of person he described fits your description."

"Why my description and not yours? You're trying to get rid of him so you can have your life back. You know my life is swamped with work, school, and church. I barely have time to sleep. There is no time in my life to devote myself to a guy that is looking for a wife. You know I want to graduate from college and start my career as a nurse first. Then I believe God will send me a Christian husband."

Maria said, "He didn't describe me. Mom, Dad and Lena are my witnesses."

Lena is one of Maria's two sisters. Maria was the oldest. She and I were 20 years old. Lena was 17 years old. Maria's youngest sister was 14 years old, and she had two brothers. They were 11-year-old identical twins. No matter how hard I tried, I could not tell them apart.

I said to Maria, "We need to focus on studying for our math test."

"Will you meet him? Please?" she asked.

I took a deep breath and said, "Maybe one day." I began to shuffle the pages of my math homework. Then I asked her a math question. Finally, we began to focus on math.

Maria did not give up. A week later she brought Lena to my apartment with her. I was happy to see Lena. I had not seen her since their grandmother went out of town three months before. We sat and watched "America's Funniest Home Videos" for thirty minutes. It was one of the funniest shows on television. We laughed the whole time. When the show was over, the television became background noise as we began to talk. I soon realized Maria brought Lena with her to help talk me into meeting the guy staying there. Lena was more enthusiastic about me meeting him than Maria.

She said, "Doretha, I want you to meet him. His name is Willie. He is 27 years old and talks about the Bible, church and God more than you. He reminds us of you. He is a Youth Sunday School teacher. He said to Maria, Mom, Dad and I that he asked God to bless him with an independent woman that loves God. He also described her as tall, slender, long hair, and with your skin complexion."

I said to Lena, "I told Maria I will meet him one day. Why so much pressure?"

Lena said, "You will see why once you meet him."

I told them, "I will pray about it."

They both sighed with relief. To this day, I can picture their joyous faces, as if my answer was yes. I prayed and, as a result, I looked forward to meeting Willie. Two days later, on a Tuesday night, after I arrived home from Bible study at my church. Maria called.

She said, "Doretha, if your answer is yes, Willie would like to meet you Thursday evening at seven."

After taking a deep breath, I said, "Yes, I will meet him. I'm not scheduled to work on Thursday that will be fine."

Maria said, "Yes! Hold on."

"OK," I responded.

I think she tried to put her hand over the mouth of her telephone so I could not hear her, but I overheard her yell with excitement. "Good news everybody. Doretha said 'yes, she will meet Willie'."

I heard cheers and chatter in the background. She returned to the phone trying to sound calm. She asked, "Where do you want to meet him? My Mom said you can meet him here if you want too."

"OK, I'll meet him at your house."

Maria replied with enthusiasm, "Excellent. I'll see you tomorrow at school. Have a good night."

"Good night Maria," I said, hanging up the phone. After hanging up, I thought, "I'm only meeting him. I will be honest with him and say, "I am not ready to date, but if you want to talk about the Bible, God, and church, I am okay with it." If he is looking for more, I cannot be more than a friend."

Thursday evening arrived, and I went to Maria's house at 6:30. I hoped to visit with Maria's family before Willie arrived, but everyone was gone except for Maria.

"Where's the rest of your family?" I asked.

She said, "They went out to dinner and a movie."

I had assumed everyone would be home, or, at least, Lena or her mom. I hadn't seen her whole family in three months.

Maria said, "Willie is excited to meet you. Are you excited?"

"I'm not excited, but I am curious about meeting him. Neither Lena nor you described how he looks. Is he tall or short?"

She smiled and said, "Tall."

It was obvious Maria was happy the moment finally arrived for me to meet him. I will never forget that day. He arrived promptly at seven. It was pouring rain outside. He walked up to Maria's sliding glass door where the family room was located. Maria and I were in the family room. I was sitting on the couch. Maria invited him in. He entered and stood like a soldier on the indoor floor mat. He was wearing a long army green camouflaged raincoat, navy blue pants, and black rain boots. He had a smile big as Texas; it was contagious. I couldn't help but smile back at him.

Maria smiled and said, "Hello, Willie this is my friend Doretha, Doretha this is Willie."

I stood up, walked up to him because it was obvious that he did not want to step off of the door mat and cause water to drip from his raincoat and boots onto Maria's tile floor. He reached out to shake my hand. He was tall, but I could not tell if he was thick or thin due to the large raincoat.

"Hello Doretha," he said. "I'm pleased to meet you. Maria has told me a lot about you." He continued to smile from ear to ear.

I said, "I'm pleased to meet you as well." During our introduction, out of the corner of my eye, I watched Maria leave the family room. I thought to myself, *Where on earth is she going and why is she leaving me here by myself with this happy faced man standing on her doormat?*

I quickly turned to face him and said, "Hello, Maria told me that you are staying in her grandmother's house until her grandmother returns."

He clapped his hands together one time, held them together and said, "Yes, I am." He had a real jolly southern accent. He sounded like he was from the heart of South Carolina.

I asked, "Are you originally from this area?"

"Yes, I am. Are you originally from this area?" he said, returning the question.

"Yes," as I scanned the area to see if I could spot Maria.

We both stood speechless. He continued to look at me and smile. Obviously, he was happy. I did not know what else to say. I felt awkward standing at the glass door with a stranger in someone else's home.

He kindly asked, "May I have your telephone number. I would like to call you. Maybe we can watch a movie together sometime soon."

I said okay, and we exchanged phone numbers.

He said, "I will call you soon." He reached out his hand and gently shook my hand. He turned and opened the sliding glass door to leave. His smile never ceased as he said to me, "Please tell Maria I said thank you and that I will talk to her soon."

I said, "I will tell her. You have a good night."

He said, as he walked fading into the night towards Maria's grandmother's house, "Good night."

I quickly closed and locked the glass door. I said in a loud, but subtle tone, "Maria, where are you?"

She stepped from behind a wall and said, "I am here."

I asked her, "Why did you leave me here alone in the family room with him?"

"I was standing behind the wall in the hallway. I wanted to give the two of you some privacy, even though I was eavesdropping behind the wall."

She started laughing. I laughed with her. She carried on, "So, what do you think about him?"

"I don't know yet. As you overheard, I gave him my phone number. I noticed he smiled the whole time."

She said, "I know, he smiles all the time."

"He did not talk my ears off," I said.

Chuckling, she remarked, "You had him speechless, that's a miracle!"

I said, "Maria, you are too funny. Tell your family that I said 'hello.' I have a lot of studying to do. I'm going to leave now."

When I left Maria's house, it was drizzling outside. On my way home I grinned from ear to ear as I thought about Willie's contagious smile and his jolly southern accent. Even though I did not have time for a serious relationship I had time for a new-found friend. If he was the way Maria and Lena described him to be, I was curious to find out more about his characteristics and attributes.

Our next chat was sooner than I expected. Willie phoned me 30 minutes after I arrived home from Maria's house. I believe he must have seen me leave her house because his call was right on time.

"Hello?" I answered.

"Hello Doretha, this is Willie. Are you busy?"

"I can only talk for a few minutes because I have homework to get done."

"What are you studying?"

"English literature. My class is having a group discussion tomorrow, and I want to be prepared for it."

"I understand," he sincerely replied. "When will you be available to watch the movie with me?"

"I'll check my work schedule and have an answer for you on Monday."

"OK, that'll be nice. I'll let you go now; I don't want to hold you from your studies. I'm looking forward to talking with you soon."

"Thank you. I know I said it to you earlier, but good night again."

"Good night," he said.

I hung up the phone and thought, He sounds like a polite gentleman. I understand why Maria did not want to say anything to make him feel bad. Instead she resorted to my apartment.

I smiled, knowing how compassionate she is about other people. Since it was late in the evening, I got ready for bed. My usual routine was to prepare for bed after work, and I then normally studied in bed. I didn't have a headboard, so my wall was my headboard. Upon getting cozy, I placed a pillow on my lap and grabbed my literature book out of the backpack on my bed. I began to study. Often I fell asleep with a book in hand and awoke at 7AM by a buzzing alarm clock. Each morning I eased out of bed and opened my blinds, turned on my worship music and prepared for my day, which started with my 9AM class. I normally had classes until 2PM and then headed to work at the retirement home for 3PM. I usually arrived at work with a song in my heart because I proudly looked forward to my work shift.

I thought about what Maria had said about Willie always smiling. I wondered why some people seemed happy about life, and some people seemed sad about their lives. I have seen sad Christians and sad non-Christians. I often wondered about one particular man, Mr. Charlie, who lived at the retirement home for years. He was tall and husky. He spoke only when someone spoke to him. His answers were always brief, and I never saw him smile. I usually greeted him on his way into the dining room for dinner.

I would ask, "Hello, Mr. Charlie how are you doing today?" His remarks were usually the same answer each time.

In a deep tone he'd say, "Well, I'm breathing."

"That's good Mr. Charlie, enjoy your dinner."

He'd respond, "Yeah," as he'd head straight towards the coffee pot to pour himself a cup of coffee before dinner was served. His routine was to have coffee with his meals. He drank about five to six cups a day and slept like a bear at night. His body was obviously immune to caffeine.

Mr. Charlie never had visitors. He rarely came out of his room other than for meals. He seldom went outside and sat alone sipping his coffee. I often wondered what was on his mind. He was one of the youngest residents there, no older than 68 years old.

One evening while doing my rounds I noticed Mr. Charlie at the snack area fixing a cup of coffee.

Being curious as to why Mr. Charlie was such a sad man, I asked, as he walked away from the snack area heading towards his room, "Mr. Charlie?"

He stopped and looked back at me, "What?"

"Mr. Charlie what happened in your life that you wish was different?" I asked.

He exclaimed in a bold, yet sympathetic tone, "My mother didn't love me. She never said "no" to me. He turned away and went to his room.

I stood there frozen in my steps at the answer he gave me. Then I gathered myself and continued my rounds checking on everyone. I thought about what he said, "My Mother didn't love me because she never told me no!" I received a life lesson from his answer. Apparently saying, "no" to a child when it is necessary helps create safe boundaries and build character. I made a promise to God that when He blessed me to be a mother, I would have the courage to say "no" to my children for their well-being and safety. I learned if a person was told "yes" all their lives, it sets them up for heartache and consequences in their future, whether from their own doing or from others. I believe that is what happened to Mr. Charlie.

The next day was Saturday. I went to work. Mr. Charlie was deep on my heart from the night before. I looked forward to greeting each resident as they entered the dining room. Dinner time was the best time to do a head count, and I had my opportunity to greet each resident and get a clue of how they were doing. I greeted them based on the unique bond we had built over the years. Each one had a special way of putting a twinkle in my eye with their words and unique personalities.

Mr. Charlie stood out like a sore thumb among the residents that evening, because of the answer he gave me the previous night about his mother. I decided to change the way I greeted him, "Hello Mr. Charlie, nice to see you today."

"I'm breathing," he grumbled as he stormed towards the coffee machine as if he was in a race.

I sighed with a confused look on my face; I thought to myself, *He didn't hear what I asked.* Obviously, the way I greeted him over the years was too routine. He answered without thinking. I whispered a silent prayer to myself, "Dear God, I pray to see Mr. Charlie in a better mood. Heal his heart. You know him better than he knows himself because you are his creator."

"So God created mankind in his own image, in the image of God he created them; male and female he created them."
—Genesis 1:27 NIV

I cared for Mr. Charlie and understood how he felt to feel unloved by a parent. It was sad to see how it affected him. His mother probably loved him in the only way she knew how. I did not know, but I knew God knew his life story and loved him unconditionally. Most likely it was too late for him to experience his mother's love but it was not too late for him to experience God's love and love from other people.

I experienced God's love at a very young age and was blessed to feel eventually my mother's love. The word "love" means a lot to me. I believe "love" is one of the most precious gifts a person can receive, experience and give.

"Love is patient. Love is kind. Love isn't jealous. It doesn't sing its own praises. It isn't arrogant. It isn't rude. It doesn't think about itself. It isn't irritable. It doesn't keep track of wrongs. It isn't happy when injustice is done, but it is happy with the truth. Love never stops being patient, never stops believing, never stops hoping, never gives up."

—1 Corinthians 13:4-7 GW

It is amazing how the love of God can heal a person's heart. I was blessed to witness and experience the characteristics of love develop in my mother as she continued to grow closer in her relationship with God. For this reason, I believed in Mr. Charlie and continued to pray on his behalf. I claimed a victorious life for him.

Over the course of a year, I began to see a gradual, positive changes in his personality. I greeted him with compassion, enthusiasm, and a smile. The day Mr. Charlie returned the smile, my heart felt like a sunflower blooming, and I sensed the angels in heaven singing, "Hallelujah!" I wanted to sing it in a high pitch tone the way I felt it in my heart. Without thinking, I clapped my hands once as an expression of what I believe was a miracle of peace in his heart. Mr. Charlie sat with others outside and talked. It was a miracle to witness the change in his demeanor and see him finally happy. I praised God that He had answered my prayer.

Yes, a year went by, and Willie and I had gotten to know one another quite well. I met him for the first time at Maria's house, and a week later he took me to the movies. I am blushing and chuckling as I am reminded of that evening. He knocked on my apartment door at 7 PM smiling from ear to ear. He was wearing a polo shirt. The top half of the shirt was a grayish color, a white horizontal stripe in the middle and the lower half of the shirt was gray. He wore black pinstripe dress pants. I said to myself, "Wow! I never saw pinstriped pants like that before." The stripes drizzled down the pants like rain drops.

"Are you ready?" I asked. The question blurted out because I was startled by how uniquely he was dressed.

"Yes, I am. You look nice," he answered with his deep southern voice while smiling.

"Thank you," I replied. I don't remember exactly what I wore. I normally wore skirts or dresses with the length below my knees, and a blouse. I believed Willie waited all week for that night because the joy that flowed out of him was contagious. Maria was correct.

He obviously loved God and was not ashamed to say, "God will always be my first love." He said it sincerely as part of our conversation that night. I knew it came from his heart. I thought to myself, I love God with all my heart, but I never heard someone say it in such a vibrant way.

I was curious to know more about what Willie knew about God. He was the youth Sunday school teacher in his church, and he reminded me often of how much he enjoyed what God called him to do. Willie grew up in a Christian home. He was the seventh child of nine children. His family were farmers. He told me a story about how they made God a priority in their lives and home.

Willie said, "My parents made sure they kept the family close together. Attending church was a priority. My parents lived by the scripture. They often stated, 'As for me and my house we will serve the LORD' (Joshua 24:15 KJV)."

Willie continued, "One Sunday morning one of my older teenage brothers tested my mother. He decided he was not going to church. Mom looked at him sitting on the couch, barefoot with his pajamas still on. As she noticed time was passing Mom said, 'Daxton we are leaving for church soon, son, why aren't you dressed yet?'

'I am not going to church today,' my brother said.

Mom replied, 'Yes, you are son.' She did not say another word as she continued doing her Sunday morning routine. The next thing I heard moments later was Mom saying, 'Time to load up in the van everyone!' She pointed at Daxton and said, 'Let's go Daxton—get in the van now.' Needless to say, he went to church with his pajamas on and no shoes.

It was clear to me that their family was serious about rules and serving God.

Willie said, "When I was eight years old my father passed away, and my mother married again. My stepfather was an amazing man, but a firm disciplinarian. He and my mother believed in raising us by biblical principles. He also had us work on the farm each evening after school until dawn. As a young boy, it was amazing to see the seeds we planted on our farm grow as we tended to them. We sold and ate what we harvested. By the works of our hands we grew many types of vegetables: cucumbers, tomatoes, melons, squash, string beans, greens, peppers, and potatoes. My favorite was the watermelon."

"And he said, So is the kingdom of God, as if a man should cast seed into the ground; And should sleep, and rise night and day, and the seed should spring and grow up, he knoweth not how. For the earth bringeth forth fruit of herself; first the blade, then the ear, after that the full corn in the ear. But when the fruit is brought forth, immediately he putteth in the sickle, because the harvest is

come." —Mark 4:26-29 KJV

Willie's childhood was obviously different from mine. However, our young adult lives were similar because we both loved God and wanted the world to know how amazing He is.

No matter what I faced in life, my trials and tribulations have become my testimony to tell all who will hear, "God answers prayers." God's desire is to lavish His love on us if we open our hearts to receive His Son, Jesus, as our personal Savior. No matter what type of life or situation we are born into God has the power to heal, restore, and reconcile our hearts. God being my Heavenly Father, having a personal relationship with Jesus, and praying to God to guide my life has always been my saving grace.

"If you ask me to do something, I will do it."
—John 14:14 GW

I was at a point in life where it was time to do some soul searching and set new life goals. While I was assessing my life, I sensed that Willie might be someone God placed along my path for a certain reason and a greater purpose. A month after we met, in a sincere tone, I reminded him, "Remember I am not looking for a relationship at this time in my life. I want to focus on God and school. We can only be friends."

He surprised me with his response, with a radiant smile, "Yes!" He exclaimed with enthusiasm as if he knew something I didn't know. "Our friendship is in God's hands, right?"

"Yes," I surprised myself and blushed when I answered. I felt our bond connecting over time, and I knew it was God drawing Willie and me closer together.

He always walked me to my apartment door after he took me to the movies or out for dinner. When he left my presence that particular evening, and I opened my apartment door, the door of my heart opened up to him as well. I decided that night to stop reminding him that we can only be friends. I realized my words could and would block the blessings of what God's plans were for my life with Willie. I reminded myself, my life is in Your hands God and You are in control.

> *"Yet I still belong to you; you hold my right hand.*
> *You guide me with your counsel, leading me*
> *to a glorious destiny."*
> —Psalm 73:23-24 NLT

We connected very well from the first time he took me to the movies. I noticed he was a gentleman with charisma. He always complimented how lovely I looked and dressed. He opened and closed the car door and every doorway we entered or exited for me. He was always polite and respectful.

About three months after our first date. One afternoon, Willie stopped by my apartment. We had no plans to go anywhere due to his work schedule. He had on his work uniform. I assumed he was on his way to work. He worked from 3 PM to 11 PM. He usually didn't stop by my apartment on his way to work. I know he didn't lose his job because he looked too excited. He worked as a facility technician. He had a college degree in electronics and we both talked about how we loved our jobs. Why he was standing at my apartment door was a mystery to me. He stood at my door obviously waiting to be invited inside. With a surprised look on my face, I said, "Hi, what are you doing here?"

"I decided to stop by to see my darling before I go to work."

"Ok." I guess I'll invite him inside. "Come in, would you like something to drink."

"Yes."

"I have cola, milk, or water."

From the couch in my living room, he answered, "Cola please, thank you."

I looked for the nicest looking glass in my cabinet to serve the special gentleman in my life with the best I had. I walked to my living room and handed it to him.

"Thank you," as he took two sips and placed the glass on the coffee table in front of him.

I couldn't decide where to sit. I didn't want to sit too close nor too far. I sat on the chair across from him on the other side of the coffee table. We were never alone in my apartment; he usually met me at my door or walked me to the door, so it was a different experience for me.

Willie seemed liked he was bubbling over with something to say. I sensed his heart was full of compassion and love as we talked. He began to talk about us. He reminded me of what he said to Maria, "You are exactly what I asked God for. You love God, and I feel the love you have for me. I was even specific with the request to God of how I wanted you to look. Your height, length of your hair and skin completion are exactly what I ask God for. He never ceases to amaze me. I thank God every day for placing you in my life. The more time I spend with you, I receive confirmation from God. I can't let another day go by without telling you that I love you with all my heart and want to spend the rest of my life with you."

Willie caught me by surprise. I did not see that coming. His words took my breath away!

Suddenly, he rose from the couch and turned towards me. Reaching into the top pocket of his uniform shirt, he took something out. Then in front of me, he knelt down onto one knee and said, "Doretha Brown will you marry me?" while holding a beautiful gold engagement ring in his hand for me.

I took a brief pause to let the reality sink in, "Yes, Willie I will marry you." Tears of joy, surprise, and excitement began to stream down my face. Willie placed the ring on my finger, and it fit perfectly.

Doretha Brown-Simmons

*"He who finds a wife finds a good thing,
and obtains favor from the LORD."*

—Proverbs 18:22 NIV

13

BEHIND THE LOVING WALLS
WE MADE OUR HOME

$\mathcal{F}$ive months later, our wedding day arrived. I reminisced about my eighth-grade dance when I wore a pink lace dress and prom night when I wore a royal blue satin dress. I felt like a princess, but nothing compared to how I felt on this special day. That day I felt not only beautiful but loved, respected, cherished, and safe. I knew both Willie and I were fashioned together by God. I felt it through the way Willie expressed his love towards me each and every day. Most of all how he loved God first.

The day was like a fairytale. I dressed next door to my church at the house of Deacon and Sister Parker. It was so convenient. Their home was beautiful, fit for a princess. I was honored when she offered to open her home as I prepared for my special wedding day. I was surrounded by the special people in my life. It was a priceless moment. They helped with my hair, nails, and wedding gown. It was a long, white, lace, gown with a train. The veil covered my face and draped down my back. With veil in place, I then slipped my feet into a pair of white, satin, high heel shoes and grabbed my purple bouquet of flowers.

Upon exiting Sister Parker's home, the long train to my dress was held up by my wedding party. As we walked towards the church, I saw cars everywhere and began feeling butterflies in my stomach. I soon spotted Harold standing in the lobby wearing a white suite. He was waiting to walk me down the aisle and give me away. His calmness helped settle the butterflies in my stomach. It was such a special moment in time. We locked arms together, and the church doors opened.

As we entered, the instrumental music, "Here Comes The

Bride" played. Everyone stood to their feet. I saw my brother Bob and many other familiar faces. I saw the joy in both my mother and future mother-in-law's eyes as they stood in their purple dresses. Their colors matched the ladies in my wedding party. The men wore white suits and purple bow ties and cummerbunds. Like proud soldiers, they stood along Willie's side. It's a precious memory that's stamped on my heart—forevermore.

As we stood together at the altar, he was dressed in an impeccable white tuxedo with a tail in the back. He wore a white bow tie and cummerbund. He looked so handsome. Pastor Simon stood waiting to marry us alongside Pastor Langston, who was Willie's Pastor. Upon reciting our wedding vows, our lives were joined by God, and we became one.

Pastor Langston did an amazing job with both Willie and I during premarital counseling. I know it sowed a good seed into our marriage. I recommend premarital counseling to everyone before getting married. Marriage is a serious vow to love and cherish each other through the best times and the worst times in life until death separates you. I was looking forward to the journey ahead for Willie and me.

I learned as a child that God is the answer to every solution, and there is power in prayer. When I thought about how God answered my prayer and restored my mother's life. Freed from the bondage of alcohol, she was serving God with all her heart. God answered many other big prayers. I was determined to keep my same faithful heart in our marriage and focus on God's plan for our life.

For our honeymoon, we headed to beautiful Orlando Florida and enjoyed a lovely time together as husband and wife. After a few days, we returned home looking forward to married life.

Upon returning to church, school and work, as a newlywed, many people asked, "How does it feel to be married?"

Smiling I'd answer back, "I feel blessed."

The majority of their responses were, "Congratulations!" or "I'm so happy for you." There were others who gave words of wisdom and advice such as: "Marriage is going to have some good days and bad days. You and Willie will need to trust in God through adversity because every marriage faces it at some point. When both of you handle it with prayer and respect, the result will reflect gloriously in your marriage." This advice came from my mother-in-law, Mrs. Rosina (Mother Rosina). I considered her a prayer warrior, and I believed she always interceded on behalf of our marriage. She was excellent at giving godly wisdom. She apparently knew the Bible because she often applied scriptures to explain what she talked about. She had years of experience as a Christian wife and parent. Mother Rosina reminded me of Maria's grandmother. She lovingly passed her wisdom down to the younger women. I took notes because I wanted to be the best wife I could be to Willie. He was a blessing and his love for God was reflected in our marriage.

Within a year after our marriage, God blessed us with our first child. A baby boy, who we named, Willie, and called Jr. He was our bundle of joy. No words could express how I felt as I held him in my arms for the very first time and counted his tiny fingers and toes.

I prayed, "God, I thank you. I promise you I will love him with all my heart. I will teach him to pray and know your ways. Thank you, God, for giving him to me, and I will trust You to help me to be the best mother I can be to him. Amen." Willie and Mom were at my bedside; it was a precious moment in time. I felt their love, compassion, and comfort on that special day. I will always cherish it.to work, attend college, and church faithfully. Being a wife, mother, and a student were a lot to juggle. I continued to remind myself, "I can do it all with God's help, faith, and strength."

Willie and I enjoyed life together and being new parents, but my mother-in-law and Willie's Pastor were correct during pre-marital counseling. Communication, praying together, and trusting God for direction in any questionable situation was vital in a marriage. We were determined to keep communication as a priority because it kept the zest flourishing in our marriage.

"…communication permits progress."

—Proverbs 13:17 TLB

Willie's smile was as contagious as it was the first day I meet him, and our love continued to grow. Jr. even had a contagious smile that attracted people to him everywhere we went. There was no doubt that Jr. was a happy baby. Willie and I took bringing a child (children) into the world very seriously. We wanted to show love and speak positive influence into their lives.

"It takes wisdom to have a good family, and it takes understanding to make it strong."
—Proverbs 24:3 NIV

We promised God when we had more children there would be no comparison or treating any child with less love. Marquel was born 21 months after Jr. The love at first sight of my babies was beyond words. Willie and I looked forward to our future with our new addition and Jr. deserved a playmate. We didn't expect life to become as busy and demanding as it did with two little children. We had to pray about some serious life changes and adjustments because they needed me at home full-time.

I made God a vow to be the best mother and wife I could be. I had to make some sacrifices to accomplish my promise. The conclusion of our prayer was for me to put college and work on hold. The heartache of walking away from two things God called me to do was painful. I knew without a shadow of a doubt God called me to care for people, and I did it on my job with a passion. I also worked diligently on my prerequisites in college to eventually apply for their registered nursing program, which was my lifelong dream. I wanted the best for my family, and I was losing hope looking through my natural eyes. I reminded myself of God's word, "For I know the plans I have for you," declares the Lord, "plans to prosper you and not to harm you, plans to give you a hope and a future" (Jeremiah 29:11 NIV).

I embraced the calling on my life and trusted God as my guide. I was grateful I followed God's direction and not my own. I was a full-time wife and mother and did it with my whole heart.

Willie and I were dedicated to being God-fearing parents. We made an oath to have self-control. We chose never to say negative things to them. We agreed not to call them words we didn't want them to become or act out. Our words were words of kindness, inspiration and encouragement. We started from day one. "I love you," was said and shown to them every day.

The following words were never said to them, even to this very day, "You're bad. You get on my nerves. You make me sick. You'll never be anything. You can't ever do anything right. Etc." We knew that negative words could break a child's heart, destroy their self-esteem and character, and even divert the plans God had for them as they grew up.

While they were still in my womb, I read the Word of God (Bible) to them. I also placed my hand on my stomach often and asked God to anoint them to be a blessing to others here on earth all the days of their lives. Willie being a youth Sunday school teacher imparted his knowledge into Jr. and Marquel before they could talk. When they were old enough to talk, then they, in turn, began to repeat what they were taught.

I believed God smiled on Willie's faithfulness as he served in church and as a husband and father. Three years after we were married, God blessed him to be ordained as a minister. He loved being a volunteer minister working along with other ministers in our community. He did it with a passion. Willie loved God first and spent a lot of time studying his Bible; it was one of the main characteristics, along with his contagious smile that attracted me to him initially.

Once married, I witnessed first-hand his close bond with God. He even took his Bible to work in his lunch box as a facility technician. Yes, in his lunch box. When Willie gave his sermons, he spoke with enthusiasm and captured our attention, which kept us wanting to hear more.

While we were in the car I would tell him, after each sermon, "Honey, I enjoyed your sermon. The message was interesting." or "You did excellent." I'd follow up with a smile and a kiss.

He'd typically answered back, "I give God the full credit,

Darling. It's not I, but Him. I'm just the vessel He is using." He always returned the smile and kiss. Willie never gave himself credit even though he spent a lot of time putting sermons together.

I did my part as a wife. I continually gave my husband the compliments he deserved. Encouraging your spouse is a special ministry part of a good marriage.

As usual, Jr. and Marquel were snuggled in their car seats in back entertaining one another as they enjoyed their after church snacks. Their snack was typically animal crackers and apple juice. They were one and two years old when Willie gave his first sermon in church.

The years went by fast. Jr. turned four years old, and I enrolled him into pre-kindergarten. Marquel was two years old. My desire was to go back to college when Jr. started pre-K. I had a little less to juggle. I believed in God to help me accomplish His will for my life. I knew He called me to be a nurse as clear as He called me to be a wife and a mother. Along with going back to college I had to keep God first, no matter how much studying I had. Going to church was a priority and a place that gave me strength ever since I could remember. I chose not to compromise quiet time with God, attending church, or my family. The first thing that came to mind was my favorite scripture, *"I can do all things through Christ who strengthens me"* (Philippians 4:13 KJV).

The day I received the college acceptance letter in the mail, Willie and I were so happy that we did a victory dance. We looked beside us to see Jr. and Marquel were dancing too; it was a beautiful sight to see. We rejoiced at the good news, and I could not thank God enough.

I completed my prerequisites for the registered nursing program and applied for the fall semester. I never checked my mailbox as often as I did that summer. I was praying and faithfully expecting good news that the nursing program would accept me as a nursing student. Every day I greeted the mail carrier at my mailbox. I never received so much junk mail in my life. The mailman noticed how I'd anxiously shuffled through the mail each summer day and by the look on my face obviously not the mail I was waiting to receive.

The word was out around school that the registered nursing program had a long waiting list, and it was very hard to get into their program. Those words went in one ear and out the other. To me, God's words had more value and authority than their words. I refused to let negative words of others cause me to doubt my destiny.

Then it happened! One day, as I shuffled through my mail, my heart thumped rapidly, and my eyes gleamed with joy.

It was obvious to the mail carrier I finally received the letter I was waiting for. "That's the letter you've been waiting for?" the mailman asked?

Bubbling up with excitement I said, "Yes, Sir!" while holding the long awaited letter in my trembling hands. I didn't waste any time opening it at the mailbox. The news I diligently prayed and worked for was in the palm of my hands. The words stood out on the page, "Congratulations, Doretha Brown you are accepted into our fall registered nursing program."

I could not get into my apartment fast enough to share the good news with Willie. I rushed to the door and whispered loudly, "Honey I'm accepted into the nursing program!" Tears of joy streamed down my face as I looked him in the eyes. Willie embraced me and whispered in my ear, "I love you, and I'm proud of you."

I laid my head on his shoulder and said, "I love you too. Thank you, God."

"Yes, Darling, God is amazing!"

I knew in my heart that God was the reason the letter was in my hand. I couldn't have done it without Him.

Next I wanted to call my mother to tell her, but Marquel was napping, and I didn't want to startle him with my excitement. So I tried quietly to phone her.

"Hello, Mom. I've been accepted into the nursing program!"

"Praise God, He is the One, who opened that door for you."

"Yes, Ma'am." We talked on the phone until it was time for me to prepare dinner. I admired my mother's life as a Christian. My faith continued to grow as I witnessed God's miraculous transformation in her life over the years.

The first day of nursing school finally arrived. I entered their auditorium, and the atmosphere was full of inspiration. I knew without a shadow of a doubt I was following my destiny. I realized it required strategic dedication and determination. I was willing to roll up my sleeves and do my best through Christ who gave me strength.

I was halfway done with school and life was going smoothly. Unexpectedly, a family emergency transpired and I found myself in the office of the Director of Nursing telling her I could no longer stay in the program. My heart broke as reality hit me. I didn't understand why I was faced with such a heart-wrenching decision. I had to choose between school and my child at home. Definitely, my child, Marquel, who was three years old, was chosen over school. He needed more of my time and care after he had surgery done to the tendons and nerves of his left arm. It was done because he had an injury that affected his left arm during his delivery process. The surgery was done to help increase his arm movement.

"Anyone who does not provide for their relatives, and especially for their own household, has denied the faith and is worse than an unbeliever." —1 Timothy 5:8 NIV

I always wanted to stay in alignment with the plans God had for my life, but I did not understand why God brought me to this hard place. There was nothing Willie could say to comfort my deep hurt. I grieved seeing my son go through so much pain, along with the loss of my dream of becoming a nurse. I laid on my bed and prayed to God because I felt like a failure. God heard my prayer because a man was on television giving a sermon that sounded exactly like my life situation.

He said, "There is someone out there today that is feeling sorry for themselves because they have failed in something that they wanted to succeed in. They feel like giving up, but you have not failed unless you have failed in your failure. Get up, brush yourself off, and try it again." He repeated that line several times, and I knew that it was directed toward me. The Holy Spirit gave me peace that surpassed my understanding and I saw myself as a registered nurse again. I refused to fail in my failure.

The man who spoke that message and gave me hope was Joel Osteen in 1999, needless to say, I got up and went back to nursing school after Marquel was well.

I had some bumps in the road on my journey in life, even during nursing school, but with God first, I persevered. I took my boards and passed the first time. In 2001, I proudly graduated from nursing school. I started working at a nearby hospital as a graduate nurse. God is phenomenal! He always leads His children in triumph. We just need to trust Him and patiently accept His timing in bringing such to completion.

Caring for people is my passion, and God gave me the opportunity to do it as a nurse. It is rewarding because I took care of every person from my heart. God blessed me with the gift to care for others, and I cherished it. Each moment I cared for others was done with compassion, no matter who they were. I considered them to be God's special creation and believed they crossed my path for a purpose. My ultimate goal was to make a positive difference in their lives.

We were trained to have empathy as a nurse, but I have tasted the salt of my tears in this career. It's hard not to when I cared for them as if they were my own family members.

I adjusted nicely in my career. Mine and Willie's love continued to grow while we were diligently involved in our church. We were dedicated to raising Jr. and Marquel, God's way. We did it by praying together and humbling ourselves before God for guidance. Our "Yes" meant "Yes" and our "No" meant "No."

Remembering Charlie in the retirement home, his misery was sad to observe. He said something to me that I will never forget, "My mother did not love me because she never told me, "No!" I promised God I would not make that mistake with my children.

Willie and I taught them right from wrong with God's word while they were very young. We had started before they were able to talk. It was our way of life. And we trusted the Holy Spirit to guide their hearts. We prayed that God would bless their childhood on into their adulthood to be all He created them to become.

"Train up a child in the way he should go: and when he is old, he will not depart from it."
—Proverbs 22:6 KJV

We noticed our way of raising Jr. and Marquel was working great. We didn't tolerate sibling rivalry. Both of them were disciplined if they did not get along. Before they were able to talk, they bonded together, and we never had a problem with them arguing with each other. The highlight was to explain to them why it was important to be respectful, kind, and caring toward one another.

I said to them, "God loves you, we love you, and God put you together as brothers to love one another. Your brother is your friend. You need each other, and that's why God gave us both of you. Love your brother at all times because if other people see you treating him unkindly, they will think they can do it also. Do you want other children to treat your brother wrong because they've seen you do it?"

With great concern in their eyes, they said, "No ma'am," as they held each other's hands.

We explained to them how important it was to always tell the truth. One of the analogies we used was *The Boy Who Cried Wolf.* Basically, what happened, a boy kept crying wolf when there was no wolf around, and people came to save him. When they arrived, there was no wolf. The boy did it over and over until no one believed him. One day the wolf showed up, and the boy cried wolf, and everyone ignored him because they thought he was telling another lie. I stressed to my sons not to lie because if your life is in danger and you do not have a solid foundation of telling the truth we can't help you. We enjoyed great communication from that day forward, and they always told the truth.

Being a close-knit family was important. We prayed and played together. We also set aside one night a week for a family night, a priceless time together. We created a lot of fond memories. Prayer was each night before bedtime and in mornings before school. Our bedtime prayer was. *"Our Father in heaven, may your name be kept holy. May your Kingdom come soon. May your will be done on earth, as it is in heaven. Give us today the food we need, and forgive us our sins, as we have forgiven those who sin against us. And don't let us yield to temptation, but rescue us from the evil one."* Matthew 6:9-13 (NLT).

Play time was a blast. Our favorite games were: Uno, Monopoly, and basketball. Besides church, our favorite places to go were the library, the park, swimming, and the zoo.

We spoke encouraging words into their life along with leading them in a positive direction. We led by example with tender, loving care. Willie and I wanted Jr. and Marquel to feel loved. We never yelled or scorned them as a way of discipline. We depended on God for direction daily on what to say and how to say it to them. We could not have done it without God being first in our life.

I remembered when I was a child it hurt to have my mother discipline me with anger and rage. I considered myself blessed because God healed her and showed her how to love Jr. and Marquel. She was a gentle and caring grandmother.

Harold and Mother went to church with us on Sundays. We journeyed together in our white minivan and had a great time of fellowship. Harold was quiet but bonded great with Willie and my two sons. Willie had a way of sparking conversations with him. Harold was known as the nice grandfather who gave Jr. and Marquel an allowance. I marveled to see my sons enjoying being around their grandparents and thanked God for the unity within our family.

Jr. and Marquel were getting older. Jr. was in the fifth grade, and Marquel was in the third grade. God blessed us with our own home after living in a two bedroom second-floor apartment for ten years. We waited for God's perfect timing, and it was worth it.

Willie and I knew the house we would call home the moment

we laid our eyes on it. We walked through multiple homes looking for the right one, in the right place, at the right price. The model home, 2000sq ft. called The Cape Cod was the perfect type of home for us in beautiful Ellenton, Florida. Buying a home was different from filling out a leasing application for an apartment, but it was all worth it in the end. We moved in nine months later.

When we received the keys to our first home, it was an overwhelming feeling of shock and joy at the same time. We could not thank God enough. We dedicated our home to Him, realizing everything we owned belonged to God.

Upon arising from slumber I slowly walked through my home, admiring the freshly painted walls. As I opened the window blinds, allowing the bright September sunrays to shine through the house, I couldn't help but wonder what else God had instore for my family and me *behind the new walls we called home.*

"Be happy with the LORD, and he will give you the desires of your heart."

—Psalm 37:4 GW

14

Not Permanently Home, Yet

My heart is filled with amazement of the glory God has for us when we dedicate everything to Him. I'm grateful to God for all He has done in my life and the wonderful plans He has in store for my future. No matter where my dwelling place on earth is, I'll always know within my heart that I'm not permanently home, yet. Why? Because I know that Jesus Christ, my Savior and Lord, is preparing an eternal dwelling place in Heaven for my loved ones and me where God resides and we'll live, love, and laugh forevermore.

I thank God for answered prayers and for giving me the opportunity to share this part of my life with you. For those of you who have gone on this journey with me; I pray that as you close this book something on its pages has touched you in a positive way. May you grasp onto hope as you move into God's wonderful plans and purposes for your future. I pray that you will never allow anything or anyone to keep you down or from experiencing God's unconditional love and the abundant life He has destined you for.

Barbara Alpert, author of *"Arise My Daughter: A Journey from Darkness to Light"* once said, "Don't allow mistakes from your past to tie you down. Refuse to let disappointments keep you from God's next appointment. The challenges that you overcome may well be the key to someone else's victory!"

"The hope we have in Christ is an absolute certainty. We can be sure that the place Christ is preparing for us will be ready when we arrive, because with Him nothing is left to chance. Everything He promised He will deliver."

~ Billy Graham

PRAYER OF SALVATION

Father God,

I believe and confess with my mouth that Jesus Christ is Your Son, the Savior of the world. I believe He died on the cross for me and bore all my sins, paying the price for them. I believe in my heart that You raised Jesus from the dead. I ask You to forgive me of my sins. I confess Jesus as my Lord. According to Your Word, I am saved and will spend eternity with you! Help me to live a life that is pleasing to You. Amen

Name: _____

Date: _____

Supporting Scriptures:

"For God so loved the world that he gave his one and only Son, that whoever believes in him shall not perish but have eternal life." John 3:16 (NIV)

"That if you confess with your mouth, "Jesus is Lord," and believe in your heart that God raised him from the dead, you will be saved. For it is with your heart that you believe and are justified, and it is with your mouth that you confess and are saved." Romans 10:9-10 (NIV)

"And we have seen and testify that the Father has sent his Son to be the Savior of the world. If anyone acknowledges that Jesus is the Son of God, God lives in him and he in God."
1 John 4:14-15 (NIV)

Doretha Brown-Simmons

ABOUT THE AUTHOR

Doretha Brown-Simmons is an amazing, inspiring and courageous woman of faith. She resides on the West Coast of Florida, near her two adult sons and caring mother. She enjoys reading her Bible, praying for others, attending church, and is active in various ministry work concerning women. She loves building people up through God's Word and love.

No matter what she is going through in life, she always wears a welcoming smile on her face. She's tenderhearted and is adored by all who know her. One of Doretha's favorite bible verses is, "I can do everything through Christ who strengthens me" (Philippians 4:13 GWT).

Doretha Brown-Simmons

Behind The Walls, I Called Home

Doretha Brown-Simmons

Behind The Walls, I Called Home

Doretha Brown-Simmons